THE TOP
100
NAMES
OF GOD

THE TOP
100
NAMES
OF GOD

ELLEN CAUGHEY

BARBOUR
PUBLISHING

Published by Barbour Publishing, Inc., P.O. Box 719, Uhrichsville, Ohio 44683, www.barbourbooks.com

Our mission is to publish and distribute inspirational products offering exceptional value and biblical encouragement to the masses.

 Member of the
Evangelical Christian
Publishers Association

Printed in the United States of America.

CONTENTS

DEDICATION

For Andy and Hannah, with love

INTRODUCTION

Who is God? Likely, you've listened to many sermons on this topic. You've probably seen artists' representations of a benevolent father figure in the heavens or of a haloed Jesus tending a flock of sheep. And chances are you've watched the fabled Hollywood versions of Bible stories, those epics that feature an unapproachable, omnipotent Spirit as God.

But one of the easiest and most fulfilling ways to know God is to consider His names and what each one tells you about Him.

In this book, *The Top 100 Names of God*, you'll find names for God that describe:

- **Who He is**—Holy, Almighty, Righteous, the Author of Our Faith, the Beginning, and Alpha and Omega
- **What He's like**—Everlasting Father, Prince of Peace, Light of the World, Bread of Life, the Way, the Truth and the Life, the Word, and the Rock
- **Why He or Jesus came to earth (and why Jesus is coming again!)**—Anointed One, Messiah, Salvation, King of Kings, Sun of Righteousness, Bridegroom, and the Resurrection and the Life
- **What He does for you**—Comforter, Counselor, Mediator, Physician, Shepherd, Guide, Friend, and Savior.

When you consider each name and then delve into the many scripture references provided, your spiritual life is sure to be enriched and your relationship with God deepened. You'll find that each name is a window, shining a light on the timelessness of our Lord.

Within the pages of this book, you'll find the treasured names of God, passed down from the ancients to you.

ADONAI

But Abram said, "O Sovereign L<small>ORD</small>, what can you give
me since I remain childless and the one who will
inherit my estate is Eliezer of Damascus?"
G<small>ENESIS</small> 15:2

When Abram uttered these words, his relationship with God, as recorded in the Bible, was relatively new. Yet based on the evidence so far in his own life—God's leading his family from Ur to Canaan, the rescue of his nephew Lot from the four kings, and the promise by God that Abram would be the father of a great people—Abram knew there was only one God, the Lord, Adonai.

The name "Adonai" is actually the plural of Adon, which means "Lord" or "Majesty." By addressing God as Adonai, Abram was emphatically praising the One who has no equal, the Lord of lords and the Lord of all the earth. In early texts, Adonai was used in place of the sacred "YHWH," or Yahweh, since no Jew was allowed to say that most reverent word. Adonai in all its variations is used hundreds of times throughout the Bible.

Despite Abram's appreciation of the divine, the next words out of his mouth were pathetically human: "What can you give me?" Even though God had told him, "I will make your offspring like the dust of the earth" (Genesis 13:16), Abram obviously wanted concrete results, not just poetic promises. Abram would have to wait many years to hold baby Isaac in his arms, the beginning of the fulfillment of God's covenant.

To call God "Adonai" implies a personal relationship with our Lord. We can call God "my Lord" or "our Lord," but how do we know He is Adonai if we haven't called out to Him in the middle of the night, perhaps to plead for a wayward child or a more hopeful diagnosis? How do we know He is Adonai if we haven't trusted Him to lead us to the right spouse, to the right job, to the right church? Only by seeing the Lord of lords work in our lives, whether by providing concrete answers or a magnificent sense of inner peace, can we voice the word first used by this Old Testament patriarch.

God wants you to acknowledge Him as Adonai. . .but more than that, He wants to have a personal relationship with you. He wants to work in your life. He wants to be your Lord. When that happens, you will echo the psalmist: "O God, You are my God; early will I seek You; my soul thirsts for You; my flesh longs for You in a dry and thirsty land where there is no water" (Psalm 63:1 NKJV).

ADVOCATE

My little children, these things I write to you, so that you may not sin. And if anyone sins, we have an Advocate with the Father, Jesus Christ the righteous.

1 JOHN 2:1 NKJV

Just before He rose into heaven forty days after the Resurrection, Jesus told His disciples, "I am with you always, even to the end of the age" (Matthew 28:20 NKJV). Likely, at that moment, the eleven men left gazing into the clouds were somewhat confused. What did that mean? Writing years later, and divinely inspired, the apostle John provided the answer. Jesus is now our Advocate in heaven, interceding for us when we fail to follow His will.

Even if you have never entered a real courtroom, you know from countless television dramas the meaning of the word "advocate"—the legal representative presenting your case before a judge and jury. By interviewing witnesses and presenting various exhibits, an attorney or advocate tries to make a case why his or her client is not guilty. When it's time for the verdict to be read, typically the judge asks the one on trial to stand beside his or her advocate.

In the same way, Jesus is our Advocate, pleading the "cases" of His followers to His Father, standing beside us in spirit. In the original New Testament Greek text, the word *parakletos* means "intercessor."

John's interpretation was substantiated by the writer of Hebrews: "For Christ has not entered the holy places made with hands, which are copies of the true, but into heaven itself, now to appear in the presence of God for us" (Hebrews 9:24 NKJV). Paul, writing to the Romans, put it this way: "It is Christ who died, and furthermore is also risen, who is even at the right hand of God, who also makes intercession for us" (Romans 8:34 NKJV).

What John isn't saying here in 1 John 2:1 is implied nonetheless: For Jesus to be our Advocate, we have to so appoint Him first. In other words, we have to ask Him to be Savior of our lives. We have to acknowledge that He is the Son of God, who came to earth to save us from our sins.

Unlike those courtroom dramas, there are no lost cases or mistrials in heaven once you've accepted Jesus as your Savior. There is no threat of punishment, civil or criminal, and no fear that your "record" will come back to haunt you. Once you've asked Jesus to forgive you, your record is clean. When you have Jesus as your Advocate, you have the ultimate counsel.

ALMIGHTY

I am Alpha and Omega, the beginning and the ending,
saith the Lord, which is, and which was,
and which is to come, the Almighty.

REVELATION 1:8 KJV

When the apostle John heard a voice one very special Lord's Day, there was no mistaking whose it was. Loud and clear as a trumpet's blast, yet more intimate. Alone in exile, John suddenly found Jesus with him. Jesus, the One John loved more than any other. . .Jesus, whom John described just moments before hearing His voice as the Almighty.

Considering where John found himself, such a description is a powerful testimony. In AD 95, the Roman emperor Domitian had exiled the apostle to the then remote Aegean island of Patmos, a place of banishment for criminals and dissidents. For a reason which would soon be revealed, John had sidestepped martyrdom, a fate that had claimed so many other disciples. God was about to use John to pen the events of the end times, events both amazing and horrifying, which would someday be preserved as the book of Revelation.

John's description of Jesus as Almighty would surely have rankled the religious Jews of Jerusalem, whose actions he had described in his gospel account. " 'We are not stoning you for any of these [Jesus' miracles],' replied the Jews, 'but for blasphemy, because you, a mere man, claim to be God'" (John 10:33). Countering that, Paul wrote to the Colossians, "For in Christ all the fullness of the Deity lives in bodily form" (Colossians 2:9).

To John, the attributes of the Almighty were threefold: Jesus lives, He has always lived, and He will live for all eternity. In fact, the first verse of John's gospel confirmed this: "In the beginning was the Word, and the Word was with God, and the Word was God" (John 1:1 KJV). John recorded later the power of life through Jesus: "I am the living bread which came down from heaven: if any man eat of this bread, he shall live for ever" (John 6:51 KJV); "Because I live, ye shall live also" (John 14:19 KJV). Jesus as an eternal presence is described by John as One who sits on His throne, living "for ever and ever" (Revelation 4:9 KJV).

The Old Testament writers commonly addressed the "Lord God Almighty," or simply "The Almighty," or recorded proclamations by Him. It was to the Lord God Almighty that sacrifices were made; His strength in battle was praised; complaints about one's state in life were moaned to the Lord God Almighty; hopes for retribution were expressed to Him; and it is He whom we are to praise for everything in creation. Amos the prophet declared, "He who forms the mountains, creates the wind, and reveals his thoughts to man, he who turns dawn to darkness, and treads the high places of the earth—the LORD God Almighty is his name" (Amos 4:13). The Almighty promises deliverance for His people, if they will return to Him; revenge for Israel's enemies; and hope of eternal life. Job, in particular, rarely failed to acknowledge God as Almighty—and never did he despise the "discipline" received from Him (Job 5:17). Much as John described the greatness of the Almighty, the writer of Job penned these words: "Can you fathom the mysteries of God? Can you probe the limits of the Almighty?" (Job 11:7).

Such reverence for the Almighty God is sorely lacking in the twenty-first century. We often hear God's or Jesus' name bandied about casually, His name used as a substitute for "Wow!" or an outburst of anger. Yet how often do we take the time to defend the name of Jesus? We feel embarrassed. We don't want to appear "holier than thou," or we're simply too harried to care.

Take a minute to reflect on John's reaction to Jesus when he saw Him. John wrote, "And when I saw him, I fell at his feet as dead" (Revelation 1:17 KJV). God has said, "Before me every knee will bow; by me every tongue will swear" (Isaiah 45:23).

One day we, too, will be able to meet the Almighty, our God who has always been and always will be—our God who is greater than human understanding.

ALPHA AND OMEGA

I am Alpha and Omega, the beginning and the ending,
saith the Lord, which is, and which was,
and which is to come, the Almighty.
REVELATION 1:8 KJV

Jesus described Himself as Alpha and Omega—the first and last letters of the Greek alphabet—three times in the Bible, and all of them occur in the book of Revelation. All of them were recorded by His beloved disciple, John. Because John's "assignment" on Patmos was to write about the events of the end times of this world, perhaps Jesus wanted to stress that He would always be with us. The world as we know it will end someday, but there will be another world, an eternal world that awaits believers, one that is dominated by our Lord, Jesus Christ, the Alpha and Omega, the One who has no end.

Even from Old Testament times, Bible writers recorded the timelessness of God. "See now that I myself am He! There is no god besides me. I put to death and I bring to life, I have wounded and I will heal, and no one can deliver out of my hand. I lift my hand to heaven and declare: As surely as I live forever, when I sharpen my flashing sword and my hand grasps it in judgment, I will take vengeance on my adversaries and repay those who hate me" (Deuteronomy 32:39–41).

Just as the God of the Old Testament lifted His "flashing sword" against the enemies of Israel, so Jesus, according to the book of Revelation, at the end of time will destroy those who do not acknowledge Him as Lord.

He has always been Alpha and Omega. Just as you cannot distinguish the beginning or end of a circle, so it is with God. The writer of Hebrews tells us that over the course of thousands of years, "Jesus Christ is the same yesterday and today and forever" (Hebrews 13:8).

After John recorded the destruction of the world and the judgment of those whose names were not found written in "the book of life" (Revelation 20:15), he described a new city, a New Jerusalem, coming down from heaven, "prepared as a bride beautifully dressed for her husband" (21:2). In the New Jerusalem, God or Jesus will live with His people and there will be no death, no crying, and no pain. After giving John this vision, Jesus said, "It is done. I am the Alpha and the Omega, the Beginning and the End. To him who is thirsty I will give to drink without cost from the spring of the water of life. He who overcomes will inherit all this, and I will be his God and he will be my son" (21:6–7).

As God created the Garden of Eden for the first man and woman as a perfect place, so He is creating another perfect place for those who declare Him Lord of their lives. Sin had no place in Eden, and it has no place in the New Jerusalem. Once we accept Jesus as our Savior—a gift without cost—we earn the right to live with Him.

In the final chapter of Revelation, Jesus impressed upon John the immediacy of these events. Three times in this chapter Jesus said that He is coming soon. So profoundly does Jesus want each person to declare Him Lord, and enjoy eternity with Him, that He's saying there's no time to waste. "Behold, I am coming soon! . . . I am the Alpha and the Omega, the First and the Last, the Beginning and the End" (22:12–13).

When you stop for your morning coffee at your favorite hangout, have you ever wondered about those workers who open and close the shop every day? As the "first" on the job, they make the coffee and set out fresh pastries. As the "last" to leave, they clean up the shop, restock the shelves, and make sure everything is ready to go the next morning.

There's a parallel here with Jesus as the Alpha and Omega. Every day, Jesus offers Himself to us—He's the same every day—and every day we have the opportunity to taste and see that He is good. At the end of each day, He prepares again to meet us the next morning, bright and early. Don't let another day go by without Jesus in your life. He wants to spend eternity with you.

AMEN

"To the angel of the church in Laodicea write:
These are the words of the Amen, the faithful and
true witness, the ruler of God's creation."
REVELATION 3:14

The word "amen," usually translated as, "so be it," typically signifies the end of a prayer or a declaration. But as part of Jesus' dictation to the apostle John, the word takes on another meaning. From the tradition of Judaism, "Amen" was used to describe "God, the Trustworthy King." Jesus, "the way and the truth and the life" (John 14:6), embraced that definition as well.

John was instructed by Jesus to write letters to seven churches, with Laodicea being the final one. As the "faithful and true witness," Jesus can only tell it like it was: Laodicea was suffering from lukewarm faith. Laodicea, a thriving metropolis in Asia Minor, a cultural and educational center, was not suffering from plague or drought. No, its condition was much more serious.

Turning the mirror onto this twenty-first century, the parallels between Laodicea and our society are obvious. Most of us lead fairly comfortable lives, barely aware of societal influences that lead us away from the Bible. What Jesus said to the Laodiceans stands today: The Amen (our trustworthy God) is waiting for you to answer His call.

ANCIENT OF DAYS

As I looked, thrones were set in place, and the Ancient of Days took his seat. His clothing was as white as snow; the hair of his head was white like wool. His throne was flaming with fire, and its wheels were all ablaze.

DANIEL 7:9

Like John, the Old Testament prophet Daniel was given a vision by God of the end times. He wasn't exiled on a lonely island, but he had been taken away from his homeland to the courts of Babylon as part of the legendary Babylonian captivity. There he spent his entire adult life, interpreting dreams and becoming a trusted advisor to kings, all the while maintaining his steadfast faith in God. As a very old man, he had been thrown into a lions' den because he refused to stop praying to his God—and survived.

Daniel's description of God as the Ancient of Days may have been culled from the prophet Isaiah's writings years earlier: "'You are my witnesses,' declares the LORD, 'that I am God. Yes, and from ancient days I am he'" (Isaiah 43:12–13). Knowing that God would be on His throne during the final judgment and beyond—and that He had been ruling the world since the beginning—Daniel's divinely appropriated choice of words was apt indeed. God is the Ancient of Days—He is eternal.

In Daniel's vision, despite the onslaught of four earthly kingdoms, described as beasts, the Ancient of Days remains on His throne. After the beasts have been vanquished, one called the "son of man," or Jesus, approaches the throne. "He approached the Ancient of Days and was led into his presence. He was given authority, glory, and sovereign power; all peoples, nations and men of every language worshiped him. His dominion is an everlasting dominion that will not pass away, and his kingdom is one that will never be destroyed" (Daniel 7:13–14).

Our culture has been called a "throwaway society"—we don't expect many of our consumer goods, our technologies, even our personal relationships, to last forever. Yet we know one thing for sure: The Ancient of Days *is* forever. If Jesus is Lord of our lives, one day, we'll spend forever with Him.

The kings of the earth take their stand and the rulers gather together against the LORD and against his Anointed One.
PSALM 2:2

In the Old Testament, the Lord's anointed would have been the king of Israel. Consider Samuel's anointing of David: "Then Samuel took the horn of oil, and anointed him. . .and the Spirit of the LORD came upon David" (1 Samuel 16:13 KJV).

This verse, however, from one of the prophetic psalms, can only be describing Jesus either at His crucifixion or in the end times. While Jesus was not anointed with oil by a prophet, He was baptized, or anointed, by the Holy Spirit. John the Baptist described this scene in the Jordan River: "I saw the Spirit descending from heaven like a dove, and it abode upon him [Jesus]" (John 1:32 KJV).

Later, in a synagogue in Nazareth, Jesus preached from the book of Isaiah, reading, "The Spirit of the Lord is upon me, because he hath anointed me to preach the gospel to the poor; he hath sent me to heal the brokenhearted, to preach deliverance to the captives, and recovering of sight to the blind, to set at liberty them that are bruised" (Luke 4:18 KJV). Speaking at Cornelius's house, the apostle Peter said, "God anointed Jesus of Nazareth with the Holy Ghost and with power" (Acts 10:38 KJV).

To be anointed means to have God's presence upon you. We couldn't be any closer to Him unless we were face-to-face with Jesus.

AUTHOR AND PERFECTER OF OUR FAITH

*Let us fix our eyes on Jesus, the author and perfecter of our faith,
who for the joy set before him endured the cross, scorning its
shame, and sat down at the right hand of the throne of God.*

HEBREWS 12:2

Because of Jesus Christ, we call ourselves Christians—that is, because He is the author of our faith. Without Jesus, there would be no Christian faith. And so it makes sense that He is also the perfecter, or finisher or completer, of our faith, depending on the Bible translation you use. What Jesus has started, He will certainly see through to perfection. As Paul writes, "He who began a good work in you will carry it on to completion until the day of Christ Jesus" (Philippians 1:6).

The word "author" was used about Jesus one other time in the Bible when Peter addressed the onlookers after he and John had healed a crippled beggar in Jesus' name: "You killed the author of life, but God raised him from the dead. We are witnesses of this. By faith in the name of Jesus, this man whom you see and know was made strong" (Acts 3:15–16).

What is this faith that we attribute to Jesus? It sent Him to the cross; it heals bodies and souls; and it will one day be our passport to heaven. The writer of Hebrews explained, "Now faith is being sure of what we hope for and certain of what we do not see. . . . By faith we understand that the universe was formed at God's command, so that what is seen was not made out of what was visible" (Hebrews 11:1, 3).

And the way to obtain such faith? Paul said we need to respond to the Author's work: "Faith comes from hearing the message, and the message is heard through the word of Christ" (Romans 10:17).

Some of the rewards of such faith are peace—"You will keep in perfect peace him [who]. . .trusts in you" (Isaiah 26:3)—and confidence—"The effect of righteousness will be quietness and confidence forever" (Isaiah 32:17), with the ultimate reward being eternal life.

As the author of the Bible, Jesus wants us to read His book. He wants us to be knowledgeable about our faith. And He wants us to ask questions—so He can provide the answers. Most of all, He wants us to acknowledge Him as Author and Savior. Once we are His, we are His forever.

He said to me: "It is done.
I am the Alpha and the Omega, the Beginning and the End."
REVELATION 21:6

From the first chapter of the first book of the Bible to the final chapter of the last book, we are told God has always existed. He was there at the beginning of the world—"In the beginning God created the heavens and the earth" (Genesis 1:1)—and He will be there in the New Jerusalem (Revelation 21–22).

This sense of equating beginning with creating can be almost overwhelming, as it was to King Solomon when he penned these words: "He [God] has made everything beautiful in its time. He has also set eternity in the hearts of men; yet they cannot fathom what God has done from beginning to end" (Ecclesiastes 3:11).

When the apostle John wrote, "That which was from the beginning, which we have heard, which we have seen with our eyes, which we have looked at and our hands have touched" (1 John 1:1), he was writing as an eyewitness to Jesus. In any court of law, that's powerful testimony. For us, that's a good reason to read more.

Do you know the One who was from the beginning? When you do, you will feel the sense of eternity in your heart, the knowledge that you have been saved and will spend eternity with Him.

BRANCH

Hear now, O Joshua the high priest, thou, and thy fellows that sit before thee: for they are men wondered at: for, behold, I will bring forth my servant the BRANCH.
ZECHARIAH 3:8 KJV

The Babylonian captivity, having just ended a decade or so earlier, was fresh in the minds of Zechariah's listeners. God knew the people needed encouragement, a reason to look to the future. And so He gave Zechariah a vision of the One to come, the Messiah, the Branch.

Years earlier, the prophet Isaiah had been the first to use this name of Jesus: "In that day the Branch of the LORD will be beautiful and glorious, and the fruit of the land will be the pride and glory of the survivors in Israel" (Isaiah 4:2). Isaiah also described the Branch as coming from "the stump of Jesse," a reference to Jesus tracing His lineage to Jesse's son, David: "From his roots a Branch will bear fruit. The Spirit of the LORD will rest on him" (Isaiah 11:1–2). Later, Jesus would describe Himself as the vine, with His followers as the branches and says: "If a man remains in me and I in him, he will bear much fruit; apart from me you can do nothing" (John 15:5).

Seeing a relative suffer from a debilitating disease has led many a researcher to develop ideas that become successful experiments, which then become drugs that save lives. Yes, when ideas bear fruit, good things happen. The same is true if we follow Jesus. When we hear and accept the Word, we can then plant the seeds of salvation in the hearts of many others. The fruit never stops ripening on the Branch!

BREAD OF LIFE

Then Jesus declared, "I am the bread of life. He who comes to me will never go hungry, and he who believes in me will never be thirsty. . . . I am the bread of life."
JOHN 6:35, 48

To "break bread" with someone usually means more than sharing a simple meal. This quaint concept implies that you have begun a relationship based on trust with another.

Jesus, as the master teacher, understood the importance of breaking bread. The day before He offered Himself as the spiritual antidote for hunger in the sixth chapter of John's gospel, He provided a feast for thousands. By this time in His earthly ministry, Jesus had already performed several miracles and word of His powers had spread. No sooner did He sit down to rest on a mountainside than a crowd of five thousand appeared!

While His disciples despaired at their predicament—it would take eight months' wages to feed this mob—Jesus had the situation in hand. With five small barley loaves and two small fish provided by a boy, Jesus blessed the food and fed the hungry throng. When appetites had been sated, there were enough leftovers to fill twelve baskets.

The next day, Jesus followed up this miracle with the spiritual interpretation: He is the Bread of Life. He was like the manna God provided for the wandering Hebrews, but He was much more. Unlike that bread—which would spoil after a day—Jesus' gift, His bread, to believers is eternal life: "Just as the living Father sent me and I live because of the Father, so the one who feeds on me will live because of me. This is the bread that came down from heaven. Your forefathers ate manna and died, but he who feeds on this bread will live forever" (John 6:57–58). Moses only led the Hebrews to the brink of the Promised Land. When we trust in Jesus, we will live forever with Him in heaven.

For this to happen—eternal life based simply on belief in Jesus—Jesus first had to pay the price of our sin on the cross. "I am the living bread that came down from heaven. If anyone eats of this bread, he will live forever. This bread is my flesh, which I will give for the life of the world" (John 6:51). Jesus knew that His disciples would have preferred seeing Him miraculously "ascend to where he was before" (John 6:62), but that was not God's plan.

The concept of Jesus as the Bread of Life was hard to swallow, both for the crowds that followed Him and His disciples. You can almost hear their murmurings: Isn't this the son of Joseph and Mary? Didn't He come from Nazareth? Likely they wondered what He meant when He said, "Whoever eats my flesh and drinks my blood remains in me, and I in him" (John 6:56). Many "disciples," but not any of the twelve, no longer followed Him. Jesus knew their hearts had not been prepared by God to receive Him.

Only Peter's staunch statement of faith was recorded by John: "Lord, to whom shall we go? You have the words of eternal life. We believe and know that you are the Holy One of God" (John 6:68–69). Peter had broken bread with the Savior, he had witnessed His miracles, and he accepted Him as the Bread of Life. Peter was no longer searching for answers; he had found the One who would reserve his place in heaven.

Many of us live day-to-day, paycheck-to-paycheck. We need our daily fix of caffeine, our bagel or hard roll, and then we're "good to go"—for a while. We try to pay the bills and maybe put a little aside, all the while hoping we won't be "downsized." But life doesn't have to be that depressing. We need to seek after that which is everlasting. We need to be saved by Jesus, the Bread of Life: "Salvation is found in no one else, for there is no other name under heaven given to men by which we must be saved" (Acts 4:12).

BRIDEGROOM

Jesus answered, "How can the guests of the bridegroom mourn while he is with them? The time will come when the bridegroom will be taken from them; then they will fast."

MATTHEW 9:15

Married or single, all Christians one day will meet their Bridegroom, Jesus. As part of Jesus' church, also known as the bride, a great ceremony awaits us in heaven where we will worship God with acclaim and jubilation (Revelation 19:6–8).

But that's getting ahead of the love story. Way back in the book of Isaiah, Jesus was introduced as the Bridegroom: "As a bridegroom rejoices over his bride, so will your God rejoice over you" (Isaiah 62:5). During Jesus' earthly ministry, He used the image of Himself as Bridegroom in parables. In the Matthew 9 passage, Jesus is foretelling His crucifixion; in the parable of the ten virgins (Matthew 25:1–13), He is cautioning believers, or His church, to be alert for His Second Coming. After Jesus began preaching, John the Baptist used the imagery, too, to deflect interest away from himself: "The bride belongs to the bridegroom. The friend who attends the bridegroom waits and listens for him, and is full of joy when he hears the bridegroom's voice. That joy is mine, and it is now complete" (John 3:29).

Jesus' courtship of His church has followed traditional guidelines. He chose us to be His own (John 15:16), professing His deep and abiding love: "Greater love has no one than this, that he lay down his life for his friends" (John 15:13). As all worthy ancient bridegrooms, He paid a "bride price." Instead of money or property, most significantly, He shed His blood on the cross for us. As Paul wrote, "You are not your own; you were bought at a price" (1 Corinthians 6:19–20). At the Last Supper, Jesus declared, "This cup is the new covenant in my blood, which is poured out for you" (Luke 22:20). Now Jesus awaits the arrival of His bride in heaven: "In my Father's house are many rooms; if it were not so, I would have told you. I am going there to prepare a place for you" (John 14:2).

The only step that awaits is our heartfelt consent to be His.

Think about someone you love so much you can't imagine your life without them. Every time you think of them in this way, your eyes tear up and you can barely talk. Now, if possible, multiply this feeling by several times. . .and you may begin to realize how much Jesus, the Bridegroom, loves you.

CARPENTER

"Isn't this the carpenter? Isn't this Mary's son and the brother of James, Joseph, Judas, and Simon? Aren't his sisters here with us?" And they took offense at him.

MARK 6:3

Jesus' ministry on earth lasted around three and one-half years, beginning when He was about thirty (Luke 3:23). Growing up in the first century in the small town of Nazareth as the "stepson" of Joseph, who was a carpenter (Matthew 13:55), Jesus, as the firstborn, would naturally have gravitated to Joseph's profession. That means that Jesus spent more years on earth being a carpenter than preaching! Is it any wonder that the townspeople of Nazareth were amazed? They knew Him only as a lowly tradesman.

Yes, Jesus, who was fully divine and fully human (Philippians 2:6), knew what it was like to work hard for little pay. He also knew how to appeal to the common man and woman, by using references to everyday life in His sermons. He refers to the "narrow road" (Matthew 7:14), the man who built his house upon the rock (Matthew 7:25), and His yoke, which He said is easy (Matthew 11:30). He also described Himself as "the stone the builders rejected" (Matthew 21:42).

Every job involves some element of drudgery. When you've made too many copies, wiped up too many spills, gone to too many meetings and done too many loads of laundry, think about Jesus the Carpenter. He knows what you're going through, and He wants your "burden" to be His.

CHIEF SHEPHERD

And when the Chief Shepherd appears, you will receive the crown of glory that will never fade away.
1 Peter 5:4

Peter was writing to encourage the elders of a congregation in northern Asia Minor, people persecuted harshly for their faith. The Greek word *poimen,* which has been translated "shepherd," can also mean "pastor." Although this church was struggling, they could rest assured that they were being fed by Jesus Himself and would one day be rewarded by Him.

Because raising sheep was a main source of livelihood for ancient peoples, shepherds are mentioned frequently in the Bible. Kings received instruction to "shepherd" God's people and one king in particular, David, was a shepherd. But even shepherds need leading, as evidenced when David wrote, "The LORD is my shepherd, I shall not be in want" (Psalm 23:1). Centuries later, Jesus said, "I am the good shepherd. The good shepherd lays down his life for the sheep" (John 10:11).

Yet Peter's divinely penned description has a deeper meaning. By calling Jesus the Chief Shepherd, he is saying He is shepherd over all other shepherds, pastor over all other pastors. Just as Jesus was sent by His Father, pastors are to be called by God. They are then to follow God's leading to wherever He sends them and lead their flocks to true knowledge of Jesus' saving grace. They are to be fed on God's Word and to feed their flocks accordingly.

Peter, as a pastor himself, knew what it was like to be fed by the Chief Shepherd. At Jesus' arrest in Gethsemane, the impetuous but achingly loyal Peter had cut off the ear of the high priest's servant. A short time later, though, this once boastful disciple denied three times that he was Jesus' disciple, an act foretold by Jesus. Ashamed by his own cowardice, Peter would nonetheless be reinstated by Jesus. Following His resurrection, Jesus asked the disciple if he loved Him and three times Peter responded emphatically. In response to Peter, Jesus said, "Feed my lambs," "Take care of my sheep," and "Feed my sheep." (See John 21:15–17.) Peter eventually died a martyr's death after leading many to Jesus.

When we make the decision to follow Jesus, there's no fine print to decipher, no rebate instructions to follow meticulously, no additional hoops to jump through. When we trust in the Chief Shepherd, we are simply, blessedly, His for life. Jesus said, "My sheep listen to my voice; I know them, and they follow me. I give them eternal life, and they shall never perish; no one can snatch them out of my hand" (John 10:27–28).

THE CHRIST

And Jacob the father of Joseph, the husband of Mary,
of whom was born Jesus, who is called Christ.
MATTHEW 1:16

What's the purpose of having the genealogy of Jesus besides making our eyes get blurry? There are several reasons, but the most important may be that Jesus' lineage proves, in part, that He is the Christ. To be called the Christ, from the Greek *Christos,* meaning "the Anointed One," was another way of saying that Jesus was the long-awaited Messiah.

First, the Messiah was to come from the tribe of Judah, a prophecy described in the book of Genesis: "The scepter will not depart from Judah, nor the ruler's staff from between his feet, until he comes to whom it belongs and the obedience of the nations is his" (Genesis 49:10). Matthew 1:2–3 and Luke 3:29 confirm that Jesus was of the tribe of Judah.

The prophet Jeremiah foretold that the Messiah would be directly related to David: " 'The days are coming,' declares the LORD, 'when I will raise up to David a righteous Branch, a King who will reign wisely....This is the name by which he will be called: The LORD Our Righteousness'" (Jeremiah 23:5–6). A quick glance at Matthew 1:6 and Luke 3:31 confirm that Jesus as a man had descended from King David.

Still, those two pieces of evidence are not enough to erase doubt. Jesus Himself said others would present themselves as "the Christ," but that we, as true believers, are not to be deceived (Matthew 24:23). So what else was prophesied that confirms Jesus as the Christ?

For starters, the prophet Micah described the site of Jesus' birth: "But you, Bethlehem Ephrathah, though you are small among the clans of Judah, out of you will come for me one who will be ruler over Israel, whose origins are from of old, from ancient times" (Micah 5:2).

Another prophet, Zechariah, described Jesus' triumphal entry into Jerusalem on what is now known as Palm Sunday: "See, your king comes to you, righteous and having salvation, gentle and riding on a donkey" (Zechariah 9:9).

In one of his psalms, David described intimate details of what would be Jesus' crucifixion: water would pour out from Jesus; His feet and hands would be pierced; none of Jesus' bones would be broken; and that lots would be cast for His clothing (Psalm 22:14–18).

The prophet Isaiah is probably the best known of the Old Testament prophets who foretold the Messiah or the Christ. While Israel was undoubtedly expecting a handsome man to come from God, the prophet dispelled those notions: "He had no beauty or majesty to attract us to him, nothing in his appearance that we should desire him" (Isaiah 53:2). Although no accurate paintings of Jesus exist, there is evidence from early writers that substantiates Isaiah's claim.

Isaiah went on to describe the healing power of the Messiah: "Surely he took up our infirmities and carried our sorrows" (Isaiah 53:4). Matthew was the first to confirm Isaiah's prophecy, even citing it in his gospel (Matthew 8:16–17).

Isaiah also described the crucifixion: "But he was pierced

for our transgressions, he was crushed for our iniquities; the punishment that brought us peace was upon him, and by his wounds we are healed" (Isaiah 53:5). All of the gospel writers described Jesus' death in detail, precisely the way the Christ's death had been foretold centuries before.

We are so conditioned to use the title "Jesus Christ" that we don't realize what we're really saying. Jesus was not just a poor Jewish man who preached about love and forgiveness in the first century. He was not simply a holy man unjustly accused and forced to die a horrible death. His birth, life, and death were all foretold by ancient prophets, as well as His Second Coming. He was the true Anointed One, the Messiah, the Christ. One day all believers will have the privilege of echoing Peter's words: "You are the Christ, the Son of the living God" (Matthew 16:16).

COMFORTER

*And I will pray the Father, and he shall give you another
Comforter, that he may abide with you for ever.*
JOHN 14:16 KJV

Jesus and His disciples were passing through the city of Nain
when they encountered a first-century traffic jam. A funeral
procession was attracting more than the usual crowd, and
Jesus and His friends were swept into the melee. A young
man had died, not an unusual occurrence. But this man was
the only son of his widowed mother and now she was left
desolate. Luke wrote, "And when the Lord saw her, he had
compassion on her, and said unto her, Weep not. And he
came and touched the bier: and they that bare him stood
still. And he said, Young man, I say unto thee, Arise" (Luke
7:13–14 KJV).

During Jesus' ministry on earth, the picture of Jesus as
Comforter was presented many times. But Jesus' ministry
was to be brief. What John was describing in John 14:16 was
not another preacher who would come after Jesus but the
Holy Spirit. This Holy Spirit, or Comforter, from the Greek
parakletos, would comfort the disciples—and all believers—
when Jesus returned to heaven.

Jesus shared this news at what has come to be called
the Last Supper, the last Passover He would share with
His closest associates on earth. Jesus had already told them
He was going away to a place they knew, where He would

prepare "mansions" for them. The Comforter He was sending was Himself—in Spirit form and invisible to human eyes, but living inside each of them (John 14:17), a Spirit that could not come to them until Jesus had departed (John 16:7). Jesus continued: "But the Comforter. . .whom the Father will send in my name, he shall teach you all things, and bring all things to your remembrance, whatsoever I have said unto you" (John 14:26 KJV). After Peter, along with the others gathered "in one place" received the Holy Spirit on the day of Pentecost (Acts 2), Peter was able to preach so effectively that three thousand came to faith in Jesus that day.

Because Jesus has not yet returned, the Holy Spirit, or the Comforter, continues to reside in all who believe on the name of Jesus. As Peter exhorted the crowds in Jerusalem on Pentecost, "Repent, and be baptized every one of you in the name of Jesus Christ for the remission of sins, and ye shall receive the gift of the Holy Ghost. For the promise is unto you, and to your children" (Acts 2:38–39 KJV).

CONSOLATION OF ISRAEL

Behold, there was a man in Jerusalem, whose name was Simeon; and the same man was just and devout, waiting for the consolation of Israel: and the Holy Ghost was upon him.

LUKE 2:25 KJV

We often say that people "know" their Bible. That could be said of Simeon, who could probably recite Isaiah 49:13: "Sing, O heavens; and be joyful, O earth; and break forth into singing, O mountains: for the LORD hath comforted his people, and will have mercy upon his afflicted" (KJV). And without doubt, he knew Isaiah 9:6: "For unto us a child is born, unto us a son is given. . .and his name shall be. . .The mighty God, The everlasting Father, The Prince of Peace" (KJV). The Holy Spirit had told Simeon that he would not die before he had seen this very child (Luke 2:26).

When the Spirit led him to the temple in Jerusalem on this particular day, he saw Mary and Joseph, with baby in tow, who had come to give an offering of two pigeons, the amount due for their firstborn. Simeon went up to them, took Jesus in his arms and praised God, saying, "Lord, now lettest thou thy servant depart in peace. . .for mine eyes have seen thy salvation, which thou has prepared before the face of all people: a light to lighten the Gentiles, and the glory of thy people Israel" (Luke 2:29–32 KJV).

The word "consolation" comes from the Greek *paraklesis*, which means "help, encouragement, and refreshment." That definition is especially apt considering Israel's tumultuous history. Isaiah recorded the Assyrian conflict and the approaching Babylonian captivity. Following that, while a remnant of Jews returned to Jerusalem, most were scattered in the Persian Empire. As the time for Jesus' birth neared, Jews in Jerusalem were suffering under the Roman Empire and, in particular, under Herod, who had been appointed "king of the Jews."

To Simeon, under the guidance of the Holy Spirit, the child he beheld was God, come to heal, revive, and console the troubled land.

Like Simeon, we, too, have the opportunity to see Jesus, the Consolation of Israel—because He is coming again! The writer of Hebrews says, "He will appear a second time, not to bear sin, but to bring salvation to those who are waiting for him" (Hebrews 9:28). Peter says we are "to prepare [our] minds for action" (1 Peter 1:13) and Paul says those who long for His appearing will receive a crown of righteousness (2 Timothy 4:8). He's coming soon. . .are you watching and waiting?

CORNERSTONE

*Consequently, you are. . .fellow citizens with God's
people and members of God's household, built on the
foundation of the apostles and prophets, with
Christ Jesus himself as the chief cornerstone.*
EPHESIANS 2:19–20

Cornerstones on modern buildings are largely ceremonial, with civic leaders' names proudly chiseled next to the foundation date carved in Roman numerals. In ancient times, though, the stones were anything but trivial. Usually laid in the northeast corner, the cornerstone was the largest, most expensive rock that united two walls of the foundation. Great care went into picking just the right stone. The cornerstone had to be laid before the building could be built; without the cornerstone there would be no building.

Likewise, Jesus is the Cornerstone of the Christian church, for without His ministry on earth, His death on the cross, and His resurrection, there would be no church. Jesus' role as Cornerstone was proclaimed first by the psalmist, who also alluded to Jesus' rejection as the Messiah: "The stone which the builders refused is become the head stone of the corner" (Psalm 118:22 KJV).

God said to the prophet Isaiah, "Behold, I lay in Zion for a foundation a stone, a tried stone, a precious corner stone, a sure foundation" (Isaiah 28:16 KJV). And the prophet

Zechariah wrote, "From Judah will come the cornerstone" (Zechariah 10:4).

While the concept of Jesus as the foundation for the entire church all over the world may be a little overwhelming, Jesus can also be the cornerstone of our lives. To illustrate this, Jesus told a parable about the wise and foolish builders (Matthew 7:24–27). When we read the Bible or hear God's Word and then live the way Jesus wants, we're like the man who built his house on the rock. Come what may—rain, wind, and life in general—our foundation is secure. Those who don't put into practice Jesus' words are like the man who built his house on sand. When the rains and the wind came, that house fell "with a great crash." In other words, without Jesus, to use modern parlance, we self-destruct.

When was the last time you read the Bible? As King Solomon wrote, "There is nothing new under the sun" (Ecclesiastes 1:9). Any trial you're going through probably occurred somewhere in the pages of God's book. God has the answer for every situation. . .if you first cling to the rock, Jesus, the Cornerstone of the Christian faith.

COUNSELOR

*"Unless I go away, the Counselor will not come to you;
but if I go, I will send him to you."*
JOHN 16:7

Under cover of night, Nicodemus made his way to where Jesus was staying. A Pharisee and member of the Sanhedrin, the Jewish ruling council, Nicodemus was making what we would call an unsanctioned visit. As a group, the Pharisees questioned everything about Jesus. Nicodemus wanted to know more, and Jesus, as Counselor, did not disappoint.

First, Jesus told Nicodemus that he must be born again, the second time of the Spirit. When this concept proved difficult for Nicodemus to understand, Jesus shared the crux of the Christian faith in one sentence: "For God so loved the world that he gave his one and only Son, that whoever believes in him shall not perish but have eternal life" (John 3:16). Jesus' final recorded words to Nicodemus that evening are especially telling when considering Jesus as Counselor: "But whoever lives by the truth comes into the light, so that it may be seen plainly that what he has done has been done through God" (John 3:21).

Later, when Jesus encountered the Samaritan woman at the well at Sychar, He astounded her with a detailed description of her marital history, including knowledge of her present illicit relationship. To her He said, "God is spirit, and his worshipers must worship in spirit and in truth" (John 4:24).

This Spirit of truth is Jesus as Counselor. At what has come to be called the Last Supper, Jesus said to His disciples, "And I will ask the Father, and he will give you another Counselor to be with you forever—the Spirit of truth" (John 14:16–17). Jesus did not want to leave His followers without a moral compass or, more importantly, a guide to living the Christian life. To all who believe in Him, as He told Nicodemus, He promises the Holy Spirit will reside in them, to lead them in a closer walk with Him.

And why should we trust Jesus? John gives the answer early in his gospel account: Because Jesus came from God. "We have seen his glory, the glory of the One and Only, who came from the Father, full of grace and truth" (John 1:14).

This Spirit of truth, however, is not a voice of condemnation. We are not going to be berated by the Counselor, but rather, we will be encouraged to do what is right.

Jesus demonstrated this during His encounter with an adulterous woman who was being held by the Pharisees. When a large crowd had gathered in the temple courts in Jerusalem to hear Jesus teach, the Pharisees hustled the woman into His presence, trying to bait Him in front of His listeners (John 8:2–11).

"Teacher," they said, "the Law of Moses commanded us to stone such women. Now what do you say?"

Instead of accusing her, Jesus bent down and started to write in the dirt with His finger. As the Pharisees continued to needle Him, Jesus stood and said, "If any one of you is without sin, let him be the first to throw a stone at her."

One by one, the Pharisees left the temple courts, leaving

only Jesus and the woman standing there.

Still, Jesus did not condemn her even though they were alone. "Woman, where are they?" He asked. "Has no one condemned you?"

She answered, "No one."

The wisest Counselor then declared, "Then neither do I condemn you. Go now and leave your life of sin."

Because Jesus has given us this Spirit of truth, He wants us not only to lead a better life, but also to be a witness. Because the Spirit of truth testifies to us about Jesus, we must testify about Jesus to others.

We don't know much about Nicodemus, but we do know that he continued to love Jesus. He accompanied Joseph of Arimathea to collect Jesus' body after the crucifixion, bringing with him about 75 pounds of spices, as was the burial custom (see John 19:38–40). Together Nicodemus and Joseph laid Jesus' body in the garden tomb. Years later, Nicodemus is said to have died a martyr's death for his faith.

If, like Nicodemus, you have had to go against the religious traditions of your family or culture to follow where God is leading, you know the struggles he experienced. But likely, you have also experienced the rewards. Have you heard the Counselor's voice? Believe, and you will.

DAYSPRING

Through the tender mercy of our God; whereby the
dayspring from on high hath visited us. To give light
to them that sit in darkness and in the shadow of death,
to guide our feet into the way of peace.
LUKE 1:78–79 KJV

The Babylonian captivity had ended and God's people had returned to Jerusalem to rebuild the temple and restore the city gates. Like other prophets writing in this postexilic period, Malachi brought a painful message from God—but this time the focus was different. This time, instead of chastising the people for their failure to rebuild, God focused on how they were worshiping Him. The lazy priests were offering unworthy sacrifices and the men were divorcing their wives to marry younger, pagan women. Tithes and offerings were being kept for themselves and not offered to God.

Still, the Lord offered a glimmer of hope to the faithful few: "But for you who revere my name, the sun of righteousness will rise with healing in its wings" (Malachi 4:2). Four hundred years passed before that prophecy would be fulfilled, before the Dayspring first rose over the earth—at the birth of God's Son, Jesus.

A dayspring is a place of rising or the dawn. Because of God's great gift to us, the gift of His Son, we have hope and a future. Because of Jesus the Dayspring, the greatest question of life—where we will rise to spend eternity—has been answered.

DAY STAR

We have also a more sure word of prophecy; whereunto ye do well that ye take heed, as unto a light that shineth in a dark place, until the day dawn, and the day star arise in your hearts.

2 PETER 1:19 KJV

Mornings are times of promise. After nights of inky blackness, uncertainty, and fear, that shaft of light warming your face as you awake signals a new opportunity. King David understood this when he wrote, "Weeping may remain for a night, but rejoicing comes in the morning" (Psalm 30:5). Mornings are also times of prayer and praise, as we thank God for the gift of another day. Again, David wrote, "Let the morning bring me word of your unfailing love, for I have put my trust in you" (Psalm 143:8).

As the Day Star, Jesus is the bringer or bearer of light. Jesus said, "I am the light of the world. Whoever follows me will never walk in darkness, but will have the light of life" (John 8:12). When we live without Jesus, we are figuratively wandering in the dark, without purpose and without promise. But those who know Him as Savior experience the gift of morning all day, every day.

Without knowing exactly what or whom they would find, the Magi followed the star to Bethlehem, seeking to worship a newborn king. Unlike those learned men of old, we know whom we are following and we know the ending of our life journey. But what about the stops along the way? Let's wait for the Day Star to guide us.

DELIVERER

And so all Israel will be saved, as it is written: "The deliverer
will come from Zion; he will turn godlessness away from Jacob."
ROMANS 11:26

One Sabbath in Capernaum, Jesus was teaching in the synagogue when a man possessed by an evil spirit confronted Him.
Speaking through the man, the spirit said, "I know who you
are—the Holy One of God!" (Mark 1:24). With great authority,
Jesus commanded the spirit to come out of the man and the
spirit obeyed. The people who witnessed this were amazed:
Who was this Jesus, whom even the evil spirits obeyed?

This Jesus is the Deliverer, the One who has power to
keep us from evil and save us from eternal damnation. As
Paul wrote, "For he has rescued us from the dominion of
darkness and brought us into the kingdom of the Son he
loves, in whom we have redemption, the forgiveness of
sins" (Colossians 1:13–14). Writing to the Ephesians, Paul
reminds us that our struggle is not against "flesh and blood"
but rather against the "spiritual forces of evil," Satan's domain
(Ephesians 6:12).

Choices come our way every day and the wrong ones
may lead us down a slippery slope to more compromising
situations. Our Deliverer, Jesus, is more than up to the
challenge of dark forces. "In this world you will have trouble,"
Jesus said. "But take heart! I have overcome the world" (John
16:33).

*And I will shake all nations, and the desire of
all nations shall come: and I will fill this house
with glory, saith the LORD of hosts.*
HAGGAI 2:7 KJV

The rebuilding of the temple in Jerusalem had halted ten years earlier and the people were despondent. How could they equal the glory of Solomon's first temple—built with the finest materials—when they had few resources? God's message through the prophet Haggai was this: What is lacking on the outside will be more than made up for by what is inside.

Five hundred years later, into this second temple came the Desire of Nations, God's Son, Jesus. While God first brought this message to Israel, His chosen nation, the prophet Isaiah made it clear that salvation was for all peoples: "Turn to me and be saved, all you ends of the earth; for I am God, and there is no other" (Isaiah 45:22).

Today, with the click of a mouse, information can be shared around the world. Yet in this globally driven culture, Jesus is still the Desire of Nations. Instead of acknowledging our differences—as Paul wrote, "there is no Greek or Jew, circumcised or uncircumcised. . .slave or free" (Colossians 3:11)—He unites us in Him. Jesus still fills houses of worship with His glory when people, all peoples, profess His holy name.

The LORD thundered from heaven;
the voice of the Most High resounded.
PSALM 18:13

The Most High God, the God surpassing all others, is El-Elyon. Considering that many of the psalms are songs of praise, it's not surprising that the name El-Elyon is used almost twenty times in that one book of the Bible. The psalmist extolled, "There is a river whose streams make glad the city of God, the holy place where the Most High dwells" (Psalm 46:4) and at another time declared, "Let them know that you, whose name is the LORD—that you alone are the Most High over all the earth" (Psalm 83:18).

The first mention of God as El-Elyon occurs in the first book of the Bible, after the patriarch Abram defeated the four kings who had kidnapped his nephew Lot. Abram was greeted by Melchizedek, the king of Salem (or Jerusalem), who said to him, "Blessed be Abram by God Most High...who delivered your enemies into your hand" (Genesis 14:19–20).

Such sovereign power was acknowledged later by the prophet Daniel, who, after informing King Nebuchadnezzar that his royal power had been taken away, told the king, "Seven times will pass by for you until you acknowledge that the Most High is sovereign over the kingdoms of men and gives them to anyone he wishes" (Daniel 4:32).

A few verses later, Nebuchadnezzar praised El-Elyon

himself, declaring, "His dominion is an eternal dominion; his kingdom endures from generation to generation. . . . No one can hold back his hand or say to him: 'What have you done?'" (Daniel 4:34–35).

As a young girl growing up in Nazareth, an insignificant village in Galilee, Mary might have questioned El-Elyon's plans for her. But when the angel Gabriel advised her, "The Holy Spirit will come upon you, and the power of the Most High will overshadow you" (Luke 1:35), Mary responded, "I am the Lord's servant. . . . May it be to me as you have said" (Luke 1:38).

And instead of railing against God for striking him dumb during the months of his wife's pregnancy, Zechariah, with his speech restored, praised El-Elyon at the birth of his son, John the Baptist: "And you, my child, will be called a prophet of the Most High; for you will go on before the Lord to prepare the way for him. . .because of the tender mercy of our God, by which the rising sun will come to us from heaven to shine on those living in darkness and in the shadow of death, to guide our feet into the path of peace" (Luke 1:76, 78–79).

There are times when we surely have doubted God's plans for our lives. When the "perfect" job is given to another, when the child that always listened and obeyed now makes poor choices, or when a close relative or friend dies "too soon"— the list is practically endless—we may question what God is doing. At those times, and all others too, we need to trust in the God who surpasses all others. As El-Elyon, He has revealed Himself throughout the ages to all who trust in Him, and He will continue to do so.

EMMANUEL

*Behold, a virgin shall be with child, and shall bring
forth a son, and they shall call his name Emmanuel,
which being interpreted is, God with us.*
MATTHEW 1:23 KJV

The angel of the Lord appeared to Joseph in a dream, and
not a moment too soon. Joseph was on the verge of divorcing
Mary and he needed some convincing to do otherwise. First,
the angel told Joseph to take Mary as his wife because her
baby was conceived by God. Second, the angel commanded
that he, Joseph, was to name the child Jesus. And thirdly, the
angel brought news: The birth of Mary's child would fulfill
ancient prophecy. Seven hundred years earlier, the prophet
Isaiah had written, "The virgin will be with child and will give
birth to a son, and will call him Immanuel" (Isaiah 7:14).

Immanuel, the name in Hebrew, means "God with us."
The name was never meant to be Jesus' first name and in
fact is used only twice in the Bible. Rather, Immanuel is a
description of Jesus.

To the ancients, a name meaning "God with us" would
have conjured images of Old Testament Bible heroes who
knew God was with them and accomplished great things
because of His guiding hand. To Abram, God said, "I will
make you into a great nation" (Genesis 12:2) and indeed
did just that, leading him to Canaan, the future home of the
nation of Israel. God assured Abram, "I am your shield, your

very great reward" (Genesis 15:1).

To Moses, God said, "I will be with you" (Exodus 3:12), and used him as the facilitator to lead His people out of Egypt. On the long journey across the Sinai, God's presence was felt by the pillar of cloud by day and the pillar of fire by night (Exodus 13:21).

To Joshua, God said, "As I was with Moses, so I will be with you; I will never leave you nor forsake you" (Joshua 1:5) before guiding him and the Israelites into the Promised Land.

To King David, God said, "I have been with you wherever you have gone, and I have cut off all your enemies from before you" (2 Samuel 7:9). And indeed under his reign, the conquest of Canaan was completed. But David would be blessed like no other: "I will raise up your offspring to succeed you, who will come from your own body, and I will establish his kingdom. He is the one who will build a house for my Name, and I will establish the throne of his kingdom forever" (2 Samuel 7:12–13).

Although Solomon, David's son, was granted the privilege of building a temple for God, the house God was speaking of is the Church and the One whose kingdom will last forever is Jesus, our Emmanuel, our "God with us." (Jesus' earthly stepfather Joseph and His mother Mary were direct descendants of King David. See Matthew 1:1–16 for Joseph's lineage and Luke 3:23–37 for Mary's—note that Heli is thought to be Mary's father.)

As Immanuel, Jesus brings certain credentials that none of the Old Testament heroes could claim. "He is the image of the invisible God, the firstborn over all creation," Paul writes (Colossians 1:15). When He was born in the manger in Bethlehem, it was the first time God was truly among us, walking on the earth as a fully human, fully divine being. His purpose in coming was made clear by His name, Jesus: He came to save His people from their sins (Matthew 1:21).

Lastly, He will be with us not just during our lifetime but forever, once we accept Him as our Savior. Paul writes, "For I am convinced that neither death nor life, neither angels nor demons, neither the present nor the future, nor any powers, neither height nor depth, nor anything else in all creation, will be able to separate us from the love of God that is in Christ Jesus our Lord" (Romans 8:38–39).

Do you remember the first time your parents left you alone? Maybe you made the mistake of watching a scary movie on television and then were kept awake by various noises, not to mention a very active imagination. As our Emmanuel, Jesus has promised never to leave us—ever. As He said to the disciples before He ascended into heaven, "Surely I am with you always, to the very end of the age" (Matthew 28:20).

EVERLASTING FATHER

For unto us a child is born, unto us a son is given:
and the government shall be upon his shoulder:
and his name shall be called. . .The everlasting Father.
Isaiah 9:6 kjv

Glimpses from the gospels show how much Jesus loved children. Mark recorded Jesus holding a child in His arms, saying, "Whoever welcomes one of these little children in my name welcomes me" (Mark 9:37). Luke witnessed Jesus saying that the truths of the Bible were more readily accepted by children than "the wise and learned" (Luke 10:21). Jesus was also a fierce defender of children, giving one of His most savage rebukes to anyone who would lead them astray (Mark 9:42).

While we think of God as the Father, Isaiah's inspired prophecy of Jesus describes an attribute of the Messiah, one evident from His caring attitude toward children. Yet He is the Everlasting Father—His kingdom is eternal and He is the sole giver of eternal life. Speaking to John on the island of Patmos, Jesus declared Himself Alpha and Omega, "who is, and who was, and who is to come" (Revelation 1:8). To Mary, Jesus' mother, the angel Gabriel described Jesus' kingdom as one that would never end (Luke 1:33).

As a father is a creator of life, so Jesus has given us spiritual life. "He that hath the Son hath life," writes the apostle John (1 John 5:12 kjv). Indeed, when we accept Jesus as our Savior, we are born a second time. As Paul writes, "Therefore, if anyone is in Christ, he is a new creation; the old has gone, the new has come!" (2 Corinthians 5:17). Jesus Himself declares in the final book of the Bible, "Behold, I make all things new" (Revelation 21:5 KJV). All who have accepted Him as Savior can attest to the amazing transformations in their lives, not just at the moment of acceptance but from that moment onward until departing this life.

Finally, while any father is a giver of life, the best fathers are those who love their children unconditionally. "We love him, because he first loved us," John writes (1 John 4:19 KJV). Bearing the burden of the sins of humanity, Jesus gave His life on the cross so that we could be saved and live eternally with Him. We cannot (and did not) do anything to make Him love us; He simply loves us because He created us. And when we accept His gift of salvation, He loves us because we are His.

Maybe the earthly father you cherish isn't your biological one or even a relative. No matter if you call him Daddy, Uncle, Grandpa, or by his first name, the qualities this person embodies are surely those seen in Jesus. To His disciples, Jesus said, "I will not leave you as orphans; I will come to you" (John 14:18). Jesus, the Everlasting Father, is coming again to gather into His arms all who love Him back—who have accepted His gift of salvation.

FAITHFUL AND TRUE WITNESS

"To the angel of the church in Laodicea write:
These are the words of the Amen, the faithful
and true witness, the ruler of God's creation."
REVELATION 3:14

Writing to a group of persecuted Christians in Asia Minor, Peter wrote encouraging words. But he also filled his two epistles with warnings, among them one concerning "false teachers," saying, "They will secretly introduce destructive heresies, even denying the sovereign Lord who bought them. . . . Many will follow their shameful ways and will bring the way of truth into disrepute" (2 Peter 2:1–2). While false teachers occupy pulpits, the airwaves and blogs, there is still one Faithful and True Witness: Jesus.

As Jesus said when the Pharisees challenged Him: "I am one who testifies for myself; my other witness is the Father, who sent me" (John 8:18). And what is Jesus' testimony? John wrote, "And this is the testimony: God has given us eternal life, and this life is in his Son" (1 John 5:11). A few verses later, John said, "We know also that the Son of God has come and has given us understanding, so that we may know him who is true" (1 John 5:20).

King Solomon once lamented, "A faithful man who can find?" (Proverbs 20:6). We who know Jesus have found the Faithful and True Witness—and much more. Because of Jesus, we have also found the source of truth and salvation.

FIRSTFRUITS

For as in Adam all die, so in Christ all will be made alive.
But each in his own turn: Christ, the firstfruits;
then, when he comes, those who belong to him.
1 CORINTHIANS 15:22–23

To honor God after He led them out of bondage in Egypt, ancient Israelites were required to make certain offerings to Him. Among these offerings were the "firstfruits" of their soil, the best of the first crops to ripen each season (Exodus 23:19). Such offerings were part of the Feast of the Firstfruits that began the day following the Sabbath during Passover (Leviticus 23:9–14).

Now fast-forward to the New Testament. Not coincidentally, Jesus was crucified during Passover and He arose from the dead three days later. On "the first day of the week," the day following the Sabbath, *the Feast of the Firstfruits*, the women discovered His empty tomb (Mark 16:1–6).

Jesus was the best offering; He was the Firstfruits. He was the firstborn son of God, the first son of Mary, and "the firstborn over all creation" (Colossians 1:15). And, as Paul wrote in 1 Corinthians 15, He was also the first to be raised from the dead and ascend into heaven—and will at some future time return to earth to raise His followers.

Parents often say to children, "Just do your best," as if that's not an outstanding effort but an acceptable one. But to God, best *is* best. . .and the best is the firstfruits of our income, our talents and our time.

FOUNDATION

Therefore thus saith the Lord GOD, Behold, I lay in Zion for
a foundation a stone, a tried stone, a precious corner stone,
a sure foundation: he that believeth shall not make haste.
ISAIAH 28:16 KJV

Writing to the church at Corinth, Paul said that as Christians we are "God's building" (1 Corinthians 3:9). But every building needs a foundation, in effect, a prepared base on which the construction rests, and for the church of God and all believers, that foundation is Jesus Christ. Paul went on to say, "For no one can lay any foundation other than the one already laid, which is Jesus Christ" (verse 11). Centuries earlier, a psalmist wrote: "Unless the LORD builds the house, its builders labor in vain" (Psalm 127:1).

Jesus Christ provides a foundation that is of lasting and eternal value. When we profess faith in Him, He, in turn, assures us of an eternal future. Jesus said, "The words I have spoken to you are spirit and they are life" (John 6:63). With Jesus as our foundation and with the Bible as our guide, we can build meaningful lives.

The old hymn, "Standing on the Promises," contains this verse:

Standing on the promises that cannot fail,
When the howling storms of doubt and fear assail,
By the living Word of God I shall prevail,
Standing on the promises of God.

With Jesus as our Foundation, we will not be immune from trouble—but we've got a future that's unbeatable.

FOUNTAIN

On that day a fountain will be opened to the house of David and the inhabitants of Jerusalem, to cleanse them from sin and impurity.
ZECHARIAH 13:1

At a time in the future, the exact date of which is unknown except to God, Jesus will return and establish His perfect kingdom, the New Jerusalem (Revelation 21). The prophet Joel describes mountains dripping with new wine, hills flowing with milk, and ravines running with water (Joel 3:18). And, in the same vein as Zechariah, Joel wrote, "A fountain will flow out of the LORD's house and will water the valley of acacias."

Throughout the Bible, the precious commodity water and a source of it, the fountain, are associated with the quenching of thirst, both physically and spiritually, and forgiveness (the cleansing of sin). Jesus as the Fountain is the source of "living water," a gift He pours out in the form of His Holy Spirit on all who believe. As Jesus told the Samaritan woman at the well: "The water I give. . .will become. . .a spring of water welling up to eternal life" (John 4:14).

In what we used to call "westerns," those action-filled

dramas on television and in the movies, there was often a stranded cowboy staggering across an unforgiving desert with his empty canteen. That's a good picture of what we're really like without Jesus—thirsty for spiritual enlightenment and in need of salvation. Come to Jesus today and be refreshed and renewed.

FRIEND OF SINNERS

The Son of Man came eating and drinking,
and they say, "Here is a glutton and a drunkard,
a friend of tax collectors and 'sinners.'"
MATTHEW 11:19

To the Jews living under the thumb of the Roman Empire, tax collectors were pawns of their oppressors—they called them "licensed robbers." They were daily reminders that God had truly forsaken them. So great was ancient Jewry's disdain for these men that they were denied fellowship in the temple and their money was considered tainted.

In this contentious milieu, Jesus befriended two tax collectors. One, Levi (also known as Matthew), even became one of His twelve disciples. Upon calling Matthew to follow Him, Jesus said, "I have not come to call the righteous, but sinners to repentance" (Luke 5:32). Witnesses commented that Jesus was the "guest of a sinner" when He visited the home of the tax collector Zacchaeus (Luke 19:7). Later, after

Zacchaeus pledged to return ill-gotten gains, Jesus offered Him salvation.

As the Friend of Sinners, though, Jesus did not come just to redeem tax collectors. When Jesus walked the earth, He befriended the physically handicapped (Matthew 11:1–5), the sick (Matthew 14:14), the demon-possessed (Luke 4:35), and the immoral (John 4:18). He made no distinction between classes or races. In fact, in His final words to His disciples, He told them to "go and make disciples of all nations, baptizing them in the name of the Father and of the Son and of the Holy Spirit" (Matthew 28:19).

Who, then, is a sinner? Paul wrote, "There is no one righteous, not even one" (Romans 3:10). A few verses later, he stated, "Righteousness from God comes through faith in Jesus Christ to all who believe. There is no difference, for all have sinned and fall short of the glory of God" (verses 22–23). No matter our occupation or our social status, our education or our background, or the condition of our health, we are all sinners in need of a Friend—a Friend who can save us from our sins.

Such a Friend can only be one without sin Himself. "For we do not have a high priest who is unable to sympathize with our weaknesses," said the writer of Hebrews, "but we have one who has been tempted in every way, just as we are— yet was without sin" (Hebrews 4:15).

Jesus understands how and why we make poor choices. That's why He offered Himself as the ultimate sacrifice for our sinful nature. Jesus said, "Love each other as I have loved you. Greater love has no one than this, that he lay down his life for his friends" (John 15:12–13). By following Jesus, we are not called to be martyrs, but we are commanded to love those in need. In other words, we are commanded to seek out modern-day tax collectors—and all who need the Friend of Sinners.

GATE FOR THE SHEEP

Therefore Jesus said again, "I tell you the truth, I am the gate for the sheep."
JOHN 10:7

Jesus' first-century audience would have perfectly understood this metaphorical description. Shepherds in the fields routinely built crude enclosures for their sheep out of branches and stones, leaving space for a single entrance or a gate. At night, after all the sheep were safely inside the enclosure, the shepherd would sleep across the gateway, thus making sure that no wild animals or bandits entered the pen.

Jesus is the Gate for His sheep: We enter into Christian fellowship only by believing in Him. And once we cross that threshold and experience salvation, we are always His and our salvation will never be stolen or lost. Jesus said, "I am the gate; whoever enters through me will be saved. He will come in and go out, and find pasture" (John 10:9).

As the Gate to the pasture, once we belong to Jesus, we experience peace as well as receive sustenance. We want to learn more about our Shepherd, knowledge that can be gleaned by reading God's Word. And the peace we so crave is readily available by seeking Him in earnest prayer.

From the moment we enter this world, we have a need to be protected. Babies cling to favorite blankets or stuffed toys; young children hold on to a parent's hand; teenagers often travel in groups; and adults have wills and insurance. What's missing? Go through the Gate for the Sheep to find the protection that transcends human understanding, as well as deep fulfillment and peace and eternal life.

GIFT OF GOD

Thanks be to God for his indescribable gift!
2 CORINTHIANS 9:15

Jesus is God's gift to the world. John wrote, "And we have seen and do testify that the Father sent the Son to be the Saviour of the world" (1 John 4:14 KJV). Jesus was God's own presence in a human body—as Jesus said, "I and the Father are one" (John 10:30)—come to earth to show us how to live abundantly and eternally.

Jesus, the Gift of God, gave us, in turn, the gift of salvation. As Paul wrote to the church in Rome, "the wages of sin is death; but the gift of God is eternal life through Jesus Christ our Lord" (Romans 6:23 KJV). We can ask for this gift by inviting Jesus into our lives, but we can do nothing to earn this reward. "For by grace are ye saved through faith; and that not of yourselves; it is the gift of God," Paul stated unequivocally (Ephesians 2:8 KJV). Jesus is simply a gift of love from the Father ("For God so loved the world" [John 3:16]), who wants to have a never-ending relationship with us.

There are many adages that speak to procrastinators. "The early bird catches the worm" and "Don't put off until tomorrow what you can do today" are two examples. The Bible says, "Behold, now is the accepted time; behold, now is the day of salvation" (2 Corinthians 6:2 KJV). If you have never done so, today *is* the day to accept Jesus, the Gift of God.

*Arise, shine; for thy light is come, and the
glory of the LORD is risen upon thee.*
ISAIAH 60:1 KJV

Isaiah didn't have much good news for the Israelites. In fact,
the first thirty-nine chapters of his book are filled with gloom
and doom. Based on the way the Israelites were living—
perverting God's justice and turning to pagan gods—God
was clearly displeased with them. But God had not forgotten
His people. Salvation was coming! The glory of the Lord that
Isaiah described would be Jesus, God's Son, come to earth in
the image of God (Colossians 1:15).

Prior to Isaiah, Old Testament writers wrote of the glory
of the Lord, or God's presence, in the tabernacle (Exodus
40:34) and the temple (1 Kings 8:11). When a cloud filled
the structure, God's glory was there and no one could enter
or perform any official duties. Likely, Isaiah's audience was
astounded when the prophet relayed these words: "And the
glory of the LORD will be revealed, and all mankind together
will see it" (Isaiah 40:5).

From the beginning of Jesus' life on earth, an event
heralded by angels displaying the glory of the Lord to terrified
shepherds, to His resurrection and ascension to heaven, God's
glory was continually on display.

When you love and admire someone, you try to be like
them. Paul wrote, "We. . .all reflect the Lord's glory. . .being

transformed into his likeness with ever-increasing glory" (2 Corinthians 3:18). Once covered by a cloud, the glory of the Lord now transforms the faces of all who love God's Son.

GOD

In the beginning was the Word, and the Word was with God, and the Word was God.
JOHN 1:1 KJV

One Bible verse that almost everyone knows also happens to be a good introduction to God: "In the beginning God created the heaven and the earth" (Genesis 1:1 KJV). From that verse alone, God, the creator of the universe, can be seen as timeless, all-knowing, and all-powerful.

The word "God," which does not appear in the original Hebrew or Greek manuscripts of the Bible, comes from an Old English word meaning "that which is invoked." "God" is a translation of the Hebrew *El* and *Elohim*, meaning "to be strong," words used when describing the creator of the universe and the judge of the world.

God once said to Moses, "I AM WHO I AM" (Exodus 3:14 NKJV). The Bible makes clear that God is not a man (Numbers 23:19) but rather, the Spirit (John 3:5–8) that is invisible (1 Timothy 1:17) and is everywhere (Psalm 139:7–12). No man has ever seen God. In fact, when Moses went up Mount Sinai to receive the Ten Commandments from God, the mountain was covered in clouds and a murky darkness, masking God's presence (Exodus 19:16–18). The point is that God simply is who He is and He has always been the same. He had no beginning because He has always existed: "Before the mountains were brought forth, or ever thou hadst formed the earth and the world, even from everlasting to everlasting, thou art God" (Psalm 90:2 KJV). God is truly without beginning or end.

What is God like? Back we go to Genesis 1:1. As the Creator, His knowledge is so vast that it defies description, yet His attention to detail is truly staggering. As John writes, "God is greater than our heart, and knoweth all things" (1 John 3:20 KJV). So great is God's wisdom that He knows our very thoughts: "For my thoughts are not your thoughts" (Isaiah 55:8 KJV). And He knows that His words will have an effect on us. He has said that "my word. . .shall not return unto me void, but it shall accomplish that which I please" (Isaiah 55:11 KJV).

As Creator, God is all-powerful. Throughout the Old Testament, "the hand of God" was seen guiding the Israelites as they vanquished their enemies. It also punished those who defied the Almighty. Jeremiah writes, "Ah, Lord GOD! behold, thou hast made the heaven and the earth by thy great power and stretched out arm, and there is nothing too hard for thee" (Jeremiah 32:17 KJV).

God embodies holiness and goodness, patience, justice, mercy, and love. In a vision given him by God, Isaiah describes seeing the throne of God, surrounded by seraphim who cried, "Holy, holy, holy, is the LORD of hosts: the whole earth is full of his glory" (Isaiah 6:3 KJV).

Yet His lofty status in no way prevents Him from exuding compassion and goodness. David wrote, "The LORD is good to all; he has compassion on all he has made" (Psalm 145:9). All good gifts we receive are from God. James wrote, "from the Father. . .who does not change like shifting shadows" (James 1:17). Because He is so compassionate, He is slow to anger, wanting to show mercy to all (Exodus 34:6).

For that reason—wanting everyone to come to knowledge of the truth in Him (1 Timothy 2:4)—God demonstrated His overwhelming love by sending His Son Jesus to die on the cross for the sins of humanity. By accepting Jesus as Savior, we are guaranteed eternal life and thus escape eternal punishment, which is God's justice, for our sins (1 John 4:8–10). Ultimately, God is the fullest expression of love and the reason we are capable of love: "We love because he first loved us" (1 John 4:19).

There's an expression that's become a favorite of life coaches and personal trainers: "Life is not a dress rehearsal." God has given you this one opportunity to "act on life's stage"—and this one opportunity to know Him. "If. . .you seek the LORD your God, you will find him if you look for him with all your heart and with all your soul" (Deuteronomy 4:29). Make the most of your life by seeking Him today.

GOOD SHEPHERD

"I am the good shepherd. The good shepherd lays down his life for the sheep."

JOHN 10:11

Shepherding is a lonely, lowly profession. Yet those who do it must be physically and emotionally resilient, patient, strong, and brave. Sheep require constant care to do the simplest things, and the shepherd must also be ever vigilant against threats to their safety. He usually carries a rod with a crook to pull in wayward sheep and also to defend against predators.

With this job description in mind, it's not surprising that God called several men of the Bible who were shepherds and also gave Himself that name. Moses was tending the flocks of Jethro, his father-in-law, when God called him from the burning bush; David was watching his father Jesse's sheep when summoned to eventually defeat Goliath; and Amos was a shepherd in Tekoa when God gave him a message of coming destruction to take to Israel.

Contained in the psalms are well-known descriptions of God as our shepherd: "The LORD is my shepherd, I shall not be in want. He makes me lie down in green pastures, he leads me beside quiet waters, he restores my soul. . . . Even though I walk through the valley of the shadow of death, I will fear no evil, for you are with me; your rod and your staff, they comfort me" (Psalm 23:1–4); "Know that the LORD is God. It is he who made us, and we are his; we are his people, the sheep of his pasture" (Psalm 100:3).

Just before Jesus revealed Himself as the Good Shepherd, the Pharisees had been questioning Him about a miracle He performed on the Sabbath, the healing of a man born blind. First, though, they had grilled the former blind man, who stated simply, "I was blind but now I see!" (John 9:25).

Jesus answered the Pharisees, "I have come into this world, so that the blind will see and those who see will become blind" (John 9:39). Jesus knew that these Jewish religious leaders would not accept Him, but there were many, such as the blind man, hungry to know Him and believe. To them, Jesus said, "I am the good shepherd."

Hundreds of years before, Isaiah had prophesied this of Jesus: "He tends his flock like a shepherd: He gathers the lambs in his arms and carries them close to his heart; he gently leads those that have young" (Isaiah 40:11).

Note that Jesus isn't just any shepherd: He is the Good Shepherd. Unlike the "hired hand" that sees the wolf coming and runs away, Jesus willingly lays down His life for the sheep (John 10:15). The hired help cares nothing for the sheep and leaves the flock defenseless in the face of danger (John 10:12–13).

Further, as the Good Shepherd, Jesus knows His sheep and they know Him, yet there are other sheep to be added to His fold. One day there will be one flock of sheep with Jesus as its one shepherd (John 10:14, 16).

Jesus' parable isn't hard to understand. When we believe in Jesus, we follow Him, much like sheep follow a shepherd. Yet like sheep, we need constant care and guidance and often, very often, we go astray and sin. At the same time, there are those more than willing to lead us astray, the "hired hands," false teachers and other professionals, who claim to have life's answers (or tell us the answers are inside of us) and yet really don't care what happens to us. Only Jesus dealt with sin; only Jesus, who had no sin, willingly gave His life to redeem us. One day, all believers will be reunited with Jesus, our Good Shepherd, and live forever with Him.

Talk shows dominate the television listings—they're on all day. And on almost any given day, you can tune in and hear some new catchphrase that's "guaranteed" to change your life. Who's telling you the truth and who's selling you a bill of goods? Know that there are many hired hands and one Good Shepherd. There are many guides to living but only one Bible. Take the time to read God's Word and trust Him to lead you to greener pastures.

GREAT SHEPHERD

*May the God of peace, who through the blood of the
eternal covenant brought back from the dead our Lord Jesus,
that great Shepherd of the sheep, equip you with
everything good for doing his will.*
HEBREWS 13:20–21

For centuries, the Jewish people had been entrenched in
one form of worship, a worship that emphasized sacrificial
offerings, strict adherence to rituals, and limited access to
God. Now, through the book of Hebrews, they were being
asked to consider a better way to worship with Jesus at the
center, no rituals or sacrifices, and unlimited access to God.

To help the Jewish people better connect with Jesus, the
writer of Hebrews attached several titles to Him. He is one
of Abraham's descendants (chapter 2); greater than Moses
(chapter 3); a great high priest (chapter 5), one of the order
of Melchizedek (chapter 7); mediator of a new covenant
(chapter 8); and the Great Shepherd (chapter 13). Jesus, like
the Old Testament shepherds Moses and David, would be
their leader.

Jesus' role as shepherd had been foretold by the prophet
Ezekiel: "For this is what the Sovereign LORD says: I myself
will search for my sheep and look after them. As a shepherd
looks after his scattered flock when he is with them, so will I
look after my sheep" (Ezekiel 34:11–12).

Ezekiel then relayed these words from God: "I will place

over them one shepherd, my servant David, and he will tend them; he will tend them and be their shepherd" (Ezekiel 34:23). The prophet wasn't referring to David, who had already died, but to David's descendant, Jesus the Messiah.

Why does the writer call Jesus the "great" shepherd? Surely His Old Testament counterparts were great shepherds, too. Yet Jesus was distinguished by two phenomenal events that changed humanity forever: His sacrifice on the cross and His resurrection from the dead.

That sacrifice, the essence of the new and eternal covenant, would erase the burning of countless offerings and the minutiae of rituals. As God said to Ezekiel: "I will make a covenant of peace with them" (Ezekiel 34:25). It is a covenant that would give peace to our souls.

It's amazing that children develop from totally dependent babies into toddlers who declare, "I can do it myself!" The Jews of the Old Testament had to depend on the high priests to make their offerings to God and on prophets to speak God's words to them. Jesus' sacrifice and resurrection changed all that. We can now speak directly to Jesus, our Great Shepherd, anytime we want. Most importantly, we—and not through a third party—can have a relationship with Him.

GUIDE

For this God is our God for ever and ever;
he will be our guide even to the end.

PSALM 48:14

Jesus said, "I am the way and the truth and the life. No one comes to the Father except through me" (John 14:6). Jesus as our Guide was sent to earth to provide the way to salvation and eternal life. And there is only one way to salvation, as Luke recorded, quoting Paul and Silas: "Believe in the Lord Jesus, and you will be saved" (Acts 16:31).

As anyone who's ever been on a tour will tell you, the best guides are those who take care of every detail. No sacrifice is too great for them; no request is too outlandish for them to accommodate. With Jesus as our Guide—Jesus, the beginning and the end—all we have to do is trust in Him.

When we walk with Jesus as our Guide, He takes care of the details. He leads us in the light, never allowing us to stumble in the dark. Jesus said, "Whoever follows me will never walk in darkness, but will have the light of life" (John 8:12).

No sin—no wrongdoing or evil thought—of ours was too great to prevent Him from dying on the cross and then rising from the dead three days later. No request that we make prayerfully in His name, believing in Him, is too great: "Ask and you will receive, and your joy will be complete" (John 16:24).

HEAD OF THE CHURCH

*And he is the head of the body, the church; he is the beginning
and the firstborn from among the dead, so that in everything he
might have the supremacy.*
COLOSSIANS 1:18

Paul speaks of the church as one body (see also Ephesians
4:4), so it makes sense that there is only one head—and that
is Jesus. Only Jesus has been given the authority by God to
have preeminence over His church. God raised Jesus from
the dead, seated Him at His right hand in heaven, put Him
above every title that can be given and, as Paul expressed it:
"God placed all things under his feet and appointed him to
be head over everything for the church, which is his body, the
fullness of him who fills everything in every way" (Ephesians
1:22–23).

Much like the head of a company, Jesus, as the head of
the church, has delegated responsibility to those in leadership
positions—to elders and deacons, men who "keep hold of the
deep truths of the faith with a clear conscience" (1 Timothy
3:9). Every person who professes faith in Jesus Christ is a
member of the body of the church, and his or her gifts are
appointed by God (1 Corinthians 12:27–31).

Announcements from the pulpit during a worship service
often contain requests for help. There are the easy, one-time
pleas: "We need someone to bring paper cups for the children's
summer program." Then there is the more challenging variety:

"We still need a Sunday school teacher for seventh grade."

Every believer has been gifted to serve in the local church in some way. As a member of His body, how can you best serve the Head of the Church?

HIGH PRIEST

Wherefore, holy brethren, partakers of the heavenly calling, consider the Apostle and High Priest of our profession, Christ Jesus.
HEBREWS 3:1 KJV

The Hebrew Christians to whom this letter was addressed might have read this sentence again and again. Likely, they were willing to accept Jesus as the long-awaited Messiah, but Jesus as High Priest? That notion was problematic.

After the Hebrews, led by Moses and his brother Aaron, escaped the tyranny of Pharaoh in Egypt, God gave them the Ten Commandments, the laws by which they were to live. Those laws were followed by more detailed instructions for harmonious living and for the tabernacle, feasts, and sacrifices.

Some of those instructions had to do with establishing a priesthood to offer the various sacrifices, observe the rituals, and be the liaison between the Hebrew people and God. Aaron, who was Moses' brother and of the tribe of Levi, and his sons were anointed as the first priests—and God directed that this "lasting ordinance" (Exodus 29:9) of the priesthood would be for Aaron and his descendants (Exodus 29:29). From that time on, through the first and second temples in Jerusalem (until AD 70), high priests were only from the tribe of Levi.

Well aware of Jesus' lineage, the Hebrew Christians knew that He wasn't from the tribe of Levi. Jesus' earthly stepfather Joseph was a descendant of the tribe of Judah (see Matthew 1:3) and His mother Mary was as well (see Luke 3:29). How could He then be the high priest?

Like Aaron, the writer of Hebrews said, Jesus was called by God. But there the similarities end: Jesus "was designated by God to be high priest in the order of Melchizedek" (Hebrews 5:10).

Going all the way back to the book of Genesis, after Abram defeated the four kings, he gave the high priest Melchizedek, whose name means "king of righteousness," one-tenth of everything he had acquired in the war (Genesis 14:18–20). At the time of Melchizedek, there was no tribe of Levi—Isaac, the grandfather of Levi, had yet to be born!

Since Abram, the patriarch of the Hebrews, paid tribute to this high priest, it follows that Melchizedek should be considered a higher priest than Aaron. Therefore, if Jesus is a high priest in the order of Melchizedek, He is a greater high priest than Aaron.

Jesus is a greater high priest for other reasons as well. Unlike Aaron, Jesus lived a perfect life on earth—He was sinless. For that reason He was the perfect sacrifice, dying on the cross for all of our sins. And because Jesus rose from the dead and now resides in heaven, His priesthood is eternal.

"Therefore he is able to save completely those who come to God through him, because he always lives to intercede for them" (Hebrews 7:25).

"I've got your back" has become a popular expression, meaning, "Don't worry, I'll take care of you." That's what Jesus as High Priest says to us when we commit our lives to Him. He is the eternal High Priest, always there to present our case to the Father in heaven.

HOLY ONE OF ISRAEL

*"Do not be afraid, O worm Jacob, O little Israel,
for I myself will help you," declares the LORD,
your Redeemer, the Holy One of Israel.*

ISAIAH 41:14

King Sennacherib of Assyria had already captured all the fortified cities of Judah. Now he set his sights on the grand prize—Jerusalem.

There was just one problem: Hezekiah, the king of Judah, trusted in the Lord. After the Assyrian king's field commander shouted blasphemous insults outside the palace wall in Jerusalem, Hezekiah tore his clothes and went to the temple to pray.

Soon Judah's king received a message from the prophet Isaiah, a message directed at Sennacherib: "Who is it you have insulted and blasphemed? Against whom have you raised your voice and lifted your eyes in pride? Against the Holy One of Israel!" (2 Kings 19:22).

That night an angel of the Lord put to death the Assyrian forces camped outside Jerusalem, and soon after Sennacherib was killed by his own sons in the temple of his pagan god.

The Holy One of Israel, *K'dosh Israel*, is an exalted God who cannot sin and who does not tolerate sin. Not coincidentally, the name appears more times in the book of Isaiah than any other book in the Bible. When Isaiah was commissioned, he was given a vision of heaven with God on His throne and seraphim singing, "Holy, holy, holy is the Lord Almighty" (Isaiah 6:3). Isaiah knew he was in the presence of the Holy One of Israel.

Clearly, Sennacherib didn't know with whom he was dealing, and at first, Isaiah didn't either. But seeing the resplendent holiness of God caused the would-be prophet to recognize his own sinful state—and then to repent. Only then was Isaiah able to recognize God's call and say, "Here am I. Send me!" (Isaiah 6:8). You, too, serve an exalted, holy God!

HOLY SPIRIT

For prophecy never had its origin in the will of man, but men spoke from God as they were carried along by the Holy Spirit.

2 PETER 1:21

After He had been tempted in the wilderness by Satan, Jesus returned to Nazareth, His boyhood home, to preach in the synagogue on the Sabbath. The scroll containing the book of Isaiah was handed to Him and He began to read: "The Spirit of the Lord is on me..." (Luke 4:18). Previously, when John the Baptist had baptized Jesus in the Jordan River, the Holy Spirit had descended on Jesus from heaven in the form of a dove (Luke 3:22). Now the Holy Spirit was *on* Him again.

Was the Spirit a ghost, as translated by the King James Version of the Bible, or perhaps an angel, or maybe even another heavenly being?

The Holy Spirit is a person of the Trinity and was recognized by Jesus as such. When Jesus gave His disciples "the Great Commission" after being resurrected, He said to "go and make disciples of all nations, baptizing them in the name of the Father and of the Son and of the Holy Spirit" (Matthew 28:19). Much like someone can say they are a mother and a daughter, the Holy Spirit can also be considered a "role" of God and Jesus. Paul wrote that "the Lord is the Spirit, and where the Spirit of the Lord is, there is freedom" (2 Corinthians 3:17). Jesus told His disciples that He would not leave them but would come to them, that He would ask the Father to send them the Holy Spirit (John 14:16–18). The Holy Spirit is also called Comforter, Counselor, Helper, the Spirit of truth, and a Gift.

Many traits are embodied in the Holy Spirit. The Spirit is all-wise, possessing understanding well beyond our mortal grasp. As Paul wrote, "No one knows the thoughts of God except the Spirit of God" (1 Corinthians 2:11). Through the Holy Spirit, prophets in scripture were given the words of God to speak (2 Peter 1:20–21).

The Spirit embodies many gifts, which He gives "for the common good" (1 Corinthians 12:7). Among these are the gifts of wisdom, knowledge, healing, miraculous powers, and prophecy. Although the Spirit can be "grieved" by our actions, He is also known for His love (Romans 15:30). When we are bitter and angry and hurt each other with our words and actions, we also hurt the Holy Spirit (Ephesians 4:30–31). Paul advised us to be kind and compassionate, "forgiving each other, just as in Christ God forgave you" (Ephesians 4:32).

Since the day of Pentecost—fifty days after Jesus' resurrection and ten days after His ascension—all believers of Jesus have been filled with the Holy Spirit. Jesus foretold this event during His forty days on earth following the resurrection: "But you will receive power when the Holy Spirit comes on you" (Acts 1:8). Such power enabled the disciples to speak in different languages so they could travel "to the ends of the earth" spreading the words of Jesus.

From that moment until the present, the Holy Spirit has drawn believers closer to Jesus. As Jesus said, "But the. . . Holy Spirit, whom the Father will send in my name, will teach you all things and will remind you of everything I have said to you" (John 14:26). Bearing witness for Jesus, the Holy Spirit speaks only the truth, relaying the words of Jesus so that believers can bring greater glory to Him.

But how do we know what the Holy Spirit wants us to do, or where He wants us to go? As we spend time in prayer and the Word before acting, we will realize God's will for us; only then will we be able to distinguish what is true and what is fleeting—because the Holy Spirit will give us discernment. And only then will the Holy Spirit be able to lead us, as He did Barnabas and Paul (Acts 13:2), to the work for which He has called us.

HORN OF SALVATION

*"He has raised up a horn of salvation
for us in the house of his servant David."*
LUKE 1:69

It began as just another day at the temple for the priest Zechariah. When he began to burn incense at the altar, though, he found himself alone, all the worshipers having gone outside. Suddenly, the angel Gabriel appeared out of nowhere and began to speak. Zechariah couldn't stop trembling. . .what had he done to deserve this? He and his wife Elizabeth, both along in years, had lived righteous lives. The only "hiccup" had been Elizabeth's inability to have children.

Gabriel informed Zechariah that he and Elizabeth would have a son, whom they would name John, a son who would "make ready a people prepared for the Lord" (Luke 1:17). When Zechariah doubted the angel, Gabriel took away his power of speech until John was born. At baby John's circumcision, Zechariah recovered his speech and began to prophesy, praising God for redeeming His people—and for sending a horn of salvation.

This horn of salvation was not Zechariah's son, because as a priest, Zechariah was of the tribe of Levi. This redeemer was to be a descendant of David, from the tribe of Judah. Zechariah's son, who would be known as John the Baptist, would prepare the way for the long-awaited Messiah.

Animal horns connote power, and indeed Jesus brought His message of salvation with a fierce passion—and with power. Jesus as the horn of salvation had been foretold in the Old Testament: "Here I will make a horn grow for David," God says (Psalm 132:17). And the psalmist also wrote, "You have exalted my horn like that of a wild ox" (Psalm 92:10). When Jesus returns to establish His kingdom, this power will be on display for all to see.

At some point we've found ourselves hitting a brick wall or between a rock and a hard place. Whatever the euphemism for our condition, only Jesus has the strength to save us. Only He is, as David writes, "my shield and the horn of my salvation, my stronghold" (Psalm 18:2).

I AM

And God said unto Moses, I AM THAT I AM:
and he said, Thus shalt thou say unto the
children of Israel, I AM hath sent me unto you.
EXODUS 3:14 KJV

For four hundred years, the children of Israel had been living in Egypt. At first, when the patriarch Jacob's son, Joseph, was a high-ranking official in Pharaoh's palace, they enjoyed respect and prosperity. Later, though, under a different pharaoh, they were reduced to being slaves. They had come to Egypt as a people who worshiped one God, and He had not forgotten them. God heard their cries for help and He chose Moses, a child of Israel raised by the daughter of Pharaoh, to lead them out of slavery.

Speaking to Moses from a burning bush, God told him, "I am the God of your father, the God of Abraham, the God of Isaac and the God of Jacob" (Exodus 3:6). Despite that description, Moses needed further clarification before declaring himself as the leader of the Israelites. "Suppose I go to the Israelites and say to them, 'The God of your fathers has sent me to you,' and they ask me, 'What is his name?' Then what shall I tell them?" (Exodus 3:13).

Moses knew the Egyptians worshiped many gods, and he also knew that his people had been living in this culture for many generations. Would they remember God's covenant with Abram, the covenant that gave his descendants the land "from the river of Egypt to the great river, the Euphrates" (Genesis 15:18)?

And then God said that His name was "I AM." He was stating unequivocally that He was the God of Abraham, Isaac, and Jacob and that He would be their God "from generation to generation" (Exodus 3:15). God was stating that He never changes. Indeed, the name I AM is a translation of the Hebrew *Ehyeh asher ehyeh* or *Hayah*, meaning, "I am that I am" or "I will be that I will be."

Like His Father, Jesus also never changes. The writer of the book of Hebrews declared, "Jesus Christ is the same yesterday and today and forever" (Hebrews 13:8). Jesus, who has been with God since the beginning of time, will one day return to rule over His new kingdom. As God was creating Adam, He said, "Let *us* make man in our image, in *our* likeness" (Genesis 1:26, emphasis added), meaning that we are made in Jesus' image as well. And from the last book in the Bible, Jesus called Himself "the Alpha and the Omega, the First and the Last, the Beginning and the End" (Revelation 22:13).

To the Jews who questioned Jesus' assertion that He had seen Abraham, Jesus said, "I tell you the truth. . .before Abraham was born, I am!" (John 8:58). Throughout John's gospel, Jesus made several statements that started with "I am." Among other things, He said He is the bread of life, the light of the world, the door, the good shepherd, the resurrection and the life, the way and the truth and the life, and the true vine.

Traveling to ancient cultures is a mind-blowing experience. How amazing it is to walk on roads trod by Roman soldiers, to stand in the same room where Christopher Columbus received his commission to sail to the New World from Isabella and Ferdinand, or to climb up the Areopagus, or Mars Hill, in Athens, where Paul preached to the Greeks.

Yet before all cultures existed, before the earth was formed, God was and Jesus was. And Father and Son are still here, and will be forever. "I AM THAT I AM" has no beginning and no end.

JEHOVAH

*That men may know that thou, whose name alone
is JEHOVAH, art the most high over all the earth.*
PSALM 83:18 KJV

When Moses first asked God for His name, God gave him the name "I AM." And then God gave the newly appointed shepherd of His people another name. "Say to the Israelites, 'The LORD, the God of your fathers—the God of Abraham, the God of Isaac and the God of Jacob—has sent me to you.' This is my name forever, the name by which I am to be remembered from generation to generation" (Exodus 3:15).

That name, Jehovah, was a name no religious Jew living in Bible times would have dared to speak. The sacred name was never spoken aloud for fear of taking the Lord's name in vain. The English translation of the Hebrew *Yahweh*, the name Jehovah, which means "to be," would have appeared in the earliest manuscripts of the Bible as "YHWH" because ancient Hebrew contained no vowels. The exact pronunciation of YHWH, also called the Tetragrammaton, is unknown.

Empowered by Jehovah, Moses and his brother Aaron approached Pharaoh with their famous request to "let my people go." When Pharaoh answered, "Who is the LORD, that I should obey his voice. . . ?" (Exodus 5:2 KJV), Jehovah responded with a vengeance. While the patriarchs had known Him as "God Almighty," He was now known as Jehovah: He would honor the covenant He made with Abraham to deliver

His people to the land of Canaan, and He would do so with a "stretched out arm and with great judgments" (Exodus 6:6 KJV). These judgments—ten "plagues" that began with rivers turning to blood and ended with the death of all firstborn— were followed by Jehovah's dramatic escape route for His beleaguered people, the parting of the Red Sea.

That Jehovah is strong to save is a theme recorded in the book of Isaiah as well. "Behold, God is my salvation; I will trust, and not be afraid: for the LORD JEHOVAH is my strength and my song; he also is become my salvation" (Isaiah 12:2 KJV). Later, the prophet wrote, "Trust ye in the LORD for ever; for in the LORD JEHOVAH is everlasting strength" (Isaiah 26:4 KJV).

There is no record of Jesus ever using the name Jehovah— and for good reason. Scholars have suggested that had He uttered that name in the presence of other Jews, especially the Pharisees and Sadducees, He would have been subjected to extreme punishment. As God's Son, Jesus knew when He would be arrested and He chose His words carefully. Instead of Jehovah, Jesus emphasized God the Father. As John wrote, "But as many as received him [Jesus], to them gave he power to become the sons of God [the Father] even to them that believe on his name" (John 1:12 KJV).

Have you ever been introduced to someone and two seconds later forgotten his name? Or, someone talks to you and later you have trouble remembering the gist of the conversation. God, the great Jehovah, isn't like that. He heard every cry of His oppressed people in Egypt. He hears, and remembers, every word of every prayer we utter—and then He responds as only an eternal, compassionate God can. Jehovah's arm is still stretched out to save us.

JEHOVAH-JIREH

And Abraham called the name of that place Jehovahjireh: as it is said to this day, In the mount of the LORD it shall be seen.

GENESIS 22:14 KJV

The day before, the Lord had given Abraham a command, and now the aged patriarch arose early in the morning to obey. Accompanied by two of his servants, one donkey, and his son Isaac, Abraham set out for one of the mountains in the region of Moriah. Before leaving, he cut enough wood to make a burnt offering. When he saw Moriah in the distance, Abraham took the wood and his son and told his servants to stay with the donkey and wait. He said, "We will worship and then we will come back to you" (Genesis 22:5).

Abraham was on his way to sacrifice his beloved son, the only child of his wife Sarah. God had asked him to kill Isaac as a burnt offering.

As father and son continued their journey alone, Isaac's curiosity could not be contained. "Where is the lamb for the burnt offering?" he asked. And Abraham answered, "God himself will provide the lamb" (Genesis 22:7–8). The explanation satisfied the boy and they strode on.

When they reached the place God had chosen, Abraham built an altar, placed the wood he had carried upon it and bound his son, as he would a lamb, and placed him on the altar. As he raised his knife to slay his son, he heard the voice of the angel of God and he stopped. The angel—some scholars say this was Jesus' voice—told him not to lay a hand on the boy, that he had proven his faith in God. And when Abraham looked up, away from his son, he saw a ram caught by its horns in a thicket. That was the sacrifice the Lord had provided instead of Isaac. That was why Abraham called the place of the altar Jehovah-jireh: the Lord will provide.

The name Jehovah-jireh means not only "The Lord will provide" but has also been translated "The Lord will see" and "The Lord shall be seen." Indeed, the Lord saw that Abraham would obey, that his love for God was greater than it was for any thing or person, and He provided the ram caught in the thicket. Because of Abraham's unswerving devotion, the Lord shall be seen. As God told Abraham, "Through your offspring all nations on earth will be blessed, because you have obeyed me" (Genesis 22:18).

God was speaking of His own Son, Jesus. Just as God provided a ram in place of Isaac, so God provided Jesus as the sacrifice in place of all humanity. "For God did not send his Son into the world to condemn the world," John wrote, "but to save the world through him" (John 3:17). As Paul wrote, "But God demonstrates his own love for us in this: While we were still sinners, Christ died for us" (Romans 5:8). Jesus as the Lamb of God died on the cross so that we—all believers—could live eternally. For all who trust in Him, He, Jehovah-jireh, will provide.

Frequently on the news we see a political leader make an announcement, followed by the ubiquitous "Q and A" session, often cut short by a press secretary. Yet, reflecting on God's request of Abraham and Abraham's obedience, it is significant that Abraham asked no questions. All we read is Abraham's unquestioning trust in God, from the beginning of the journey to Moriah to the provision of the ram, the intended sacrifice. Abraham believed that Jehovah-jireh would provide—and He did. As Solomon wrote, "Trust in the LORD with all your heart and lean not on your own understanding; in all your ways acknowledge him, and he will make your paths straight" (Proverbs 3:5–6). Are you trusting God wholeheartedly?

JEHOVAH-ROPHE

For I will restore health unto thee,
and I will heal thee of thy wounds, saith the LORD.
JEREMIAH 30:17 KJV

Jeremiah's role as a prophet ends with the start of the Babylonian captivity, a time of tribulation he foretold throughout his book. But he had good tidings, too, words of restoration from the Lord, whom the people of Judah had forsaken. The "wounds" he was speaking of were not physical but spiritual in nature, brought on by "many sins." One day the people would be restored to their homeland and healed by the Lord, whom the prophet called Jehovah-rophe, a name that means "the Lord heals."

The name Jehovah-rophe was first used when the Israelites, just three days into their journey after crossing the Red Sea, came to the bitter, undrinkable waters of Marah. The people were thirsty and complaining, so Moses called upon the Lord. When God told Moses to throw a piece of wood into the waters, the springs became potable. And then Jehovah-rophe made a pact with the people: If you listen to Me and do what is right, I will not afflict you with any of the diseases I rained down on the Egyptians, for I am the Lord who heals you (Exodus 15:26). For the next forty years of wandering, God kept His promise.

When we're worried about our physical health, we often turn to God in prayer. Seldom are we as concerned about the state of our spiritual health. For a promising spiritual prognosis, the prescription is simple: Trust in Jesus. His healing powers, foretold by Isaiah—"By his wounds we are healed" (Isaiah 53:5)—are there for the asking. Jesus, our Jehovah-rophe, restores our spiritual health and ensures life for eternity.

JEHOVAHSHALOM

Then Gideon built an altar there unto the LORD,
and called it Jehovahshalom.
JUDGES 6:24 KJV

For seven years, the Israelites had been at the mercy of the Midianites, a people so ruthless and ravenous, scripture compares them to locusts. When they descended on the Israelites' land, they ruined all their crops "and did not spare a living thing" (Judges 6:4). Consequently, the Israelites had taken to hiding in mountain caves, out of sight of these predators. In desperation, this wayward people cried out to God and once again, He was prepared to deliver them.

To do so, God chose an unlikely candidate. By his own reckoning, Gideon came from the "weakest" clan of the tribe of Manasseh and was considered "the least" of his family. Cowed as well by the Midianites, Gideon was threshing wheat in a winepress, out of sight of the enemy, when the angel of the Lord approached him. Responding to the angel's words, "Peace! Do not be afraid" (Judges 6:23), Gideon built an altar on the very spot, calling it Jehovah-shalom.

Jehovah-shalom means "The Lord is peace" or "The Lord our peace." Through Gideon, God delivered peace to His people; through His Son Jesus and His Word, He continues to offer a balm for human souls.

"For he himself is our peace," wrote Paul (Ephesians 2:14), providing access to the Father. Because of Jesus' sacrifice on the cross and His position at God's right hand, He is able to serve as mediator for all who come to Him.

Paul also wrote of the peace Jesus brings to our hearts and minds, the peace of God "which transcends all understanding" (Philippians 4:7). Despite the troubles of the world, John told us, we still can have peace for one reason: Jesus has "overcome the world" (John 16:33).

A quick perusal of the headlines or five minutes' worth of the evening news is enough to make a person fearful. And then there are those worries closer to home, the kind that keep us up at night. At times like these, it's comforting to remember Jesus' words. "Don't be afraid," Jehovah-shalom says. "My peace I give you."

JEHOVAH-SHAMMAH

*It was round about eighteen thousand measures: and the
name of the city from that day shall be, The LORD is there.*
EZEKIEL 48:35 KJV

Ezekiel was a young man when he was taken to Babylon in
597 BC, as part of the second wave of the captivity. A few
years later, he received a call from God to hit the streets of
Babylon, prophesying and preaching. God had prepared him
for the stubborn attitudes of the Israelites, and Ezekiel was
not to be deterred. Among his messages was that Jerusalem
would be destroyed by Babylon and also that God would
bring His people back to Israel.

After Jerusalem fell, Ezekiel was directed by God to talk
about the far-distant future. The city he described, which has
a circumference of "eighteen thousand measures," is the same
one referred to by John in the book of Revelation. This New
Jerusalem "shone with the glory of God, and its brilliance was
like that of a very precious jewel" (Revelation 21:11). The glory
of God was evident because, as Ezekiel stated, the name of the
city was Jehovah-shammah, meaning "The Lord is there."

Possessions come and go and friends may drift apart or
move away—that's the nature of modern life. As believers,
though, we're blessed to have "God with us" all the time. That's
because as Emmanuel, Jesus has promised never to leave us,
giving us His Holy Spirit as our comforter and guide. Jesus,
our Jehovah-shammah, is always there.

Behold, the days come, saith the LORD, that I will raise unto David a righteous Branch, and a King shall reign and prosper, and shall execute judgment and justice in the earth. In his days Judah shall be saved, and Israel shall dwell safely: and this is his name whereby he shall be called, THE LORD OUR RIGHTEOUSNESS.
JEREMIAH 23:5–6 KJV

Jeremiah prophesied during the reigns of Judah's last five kings before the start of the Babylonian captivity. With the exception of Josiah, like most of the kings before them, they were an evil bunch, denounced by scripture as having "done evil in the sight of the Lord." Now God was promising a just ruler who was a descendant of David. The word "oxymoron" wasn't part of Jeremiah's vocabulary, but he probably wondered: *Is there such a thing as a righteous king?*

Jesus is Jehovah-tsidkenu, a name that means "The Lord our righteousness." Only Jesus, in whom there is no sin (1 John 3:5), can stand before God the Father and say that we are His. If left on our own, without a Savior, we would struggle hopelessly to follow God's laws established in the Old Testament. As Paul wrote, "No one will be declared righteous in his sight by observing the law" (Romans 3:20). Jesus is "our righteousness, holiness and redemption" (1 Corinthians 1:30).

We like to pat ourselves on the back when we "do the right thing"—almost as if it's out of character. Unlike our feeble selves, Jesus is right and righteous all the time. As our Jehovah-tsidkenu, we owe our lives to Him.

JESUS

And she shall bring forth a son, and thou shalt call his name
JESUS: for he shall save his people from their sins.
MATTHEW 1:21 KJV

Joseph woke up and knew what he had to do. Suffice it to say, he'd never had a dream like this before. In his dream, an angel of the Lord had told him to take Mary as his wife. That took care of one of his problems, in a way. Joseph was on the verge of divorcing Mary because she was expecting a baby—and it wasn't his. But then the angel told Joseph that this baby had been conceived by the Holy Spirit and that he, Joseph, was to name the baby Jesus.

This child of the virgin birth would be the long-awaited Emmanuel, "God with us," and now declared by an angel, "God has saved us."

Jesus, a name that means "salvation," is the Anglicized form of the Latin *Iesu*, which was derived from the Greek *Iesous*. The Greek form was coined from the Aramaic name *Yeshua* and the Hebrew *Yehoshua*. As the One who came to "save his people from their sins," Jesus' arrival had been foretold for hundreds of years.

Although the name *Jesus* is never mentioned in the Old

Testament, Jesus as the salvation, Yehoshua, is invoked several times. The psalmist writes, "The LORD has made his salvation known and revealed his righteousness to the nations. . .all the ends of the earth have seen the salvation of our God" (Psalm 98:2–3). And Isaiah prophesied, "Behold, the LORD hath proclaimed unto the end of the world, Say ye to the daughter of Zion, Behold, thy salvation cometh" (Isaiah 62:11 KJV).

When the devout Simeon, who had been awaiting "the consolation of Israel," is led by the Holy Spirit to the temple in Jerusalem on the very day that Mary and Joseph and the baby Jesus come to give the required offering, he also acknowledged Yehoshua. "For mine eyes have seen thy salvation," Simeon declares, "which thou hast prepared before the face of all people" (Luke 2:30–31 KJV).

The very name of Jesus is saving, and it is powerful. Jesus said, "Whatsoever ye shall ask the Father in my name, he will give it you" (John 16:23 KJV). Peter said that, "There is none other name under heaven given among men, whereby we must be saved" (Acts 4:12 KJV).

In the days of the early church, the apostles healed the sick and lame, exorcised demons, baptized, and taught and preached fearlessly—all in the name of Jesus. They knew firsthand that Jesus was no ordinary teacher; they knew that He, Yehoshua, was the Son of God. God gave Jesus a name "which is above every name," wrote Paul, "that at the name of Jesus every knee should bow" (Philippians 2:9–10 KJV).

When he awoke the next morning, scripture says that Joseph "did what the angel of the Lord had commanded him" (Matthew 1:24). He agreed to let salvation come into his house. Have you made a similar decision? Has your heart been touched by God's Word in such a way that you want to know more? Are you searching for meaning in life and getting more frustrated day after day? Jesus wants to come and live with you, too.

KING OF ISRAEL

He saved others; himself he cannot save.
If he be the King of Israel, let him now come down
from the cross, and we will believe him.

MATTHEW 27:42 KJV

The chief priests, the teachers of the law, and the elders should have known better. Yet looking up at Jesus, dying a thief's death on a wooden cross, they led the other passersby in mocking Him. But what they regarded as sarcasm was the gospel truth: Jesus is the King of Israel, and His kingdom will never end.

When the angel Gabriel gave Mary the news that she would bear God's Son, he said, "The Lord God will give him the throne of his father David, and he will reign over the house of Jacob forever; his kingdom will never end" (Luke 1:32–33). That throne of David's was the throne of Israel, and Jesus was a direct descendant of David through Mary (see Luke 3:23; Heli is thought to be Mary's father). Almost two years after Jesus' birth, the Magi confirmed His royal status, asking, "Where is the one who has been born king of the Jews?" (Matthew 2:2).

During Jesus' earthly ministry, He was acknowledged by His disciple Nathanael as the Son of God and the King of Israel (John 1:49). As He entered Jerusalem on a donkey during His last week on earth, the great crowd acknowledged His kingship, crying, "Blessed is the King of Israel!" (John

12:13). And when the Roman governor Pontius Pilate questioned Jesus before handing Him over to be crucified, Jesus admitted that He indeed was a king but that His kingdom was not of this world (John 18:36).

Jesus has promised one day to return to establish His kingdom, a kingdom in which He will reign "for ever and ever" (Revelation 11:15). Of that kingdom, the prophet Zephaniah wrote, hundreds of years before Jesus was born to Mary, "The LORD, the King of Israel, is with you; never again will you fear any harm" (Zephaniah 3:15).

Those mockers of Jesus had, in a biblical way of speaking, hardened their hearts to His message. Sometimes we do that, too. Rather than concentrate on a daily devotional reading, we're thinking about our to-do list. Or while we're supposedly listening to a Sunday sermon, we're thinking about whom we need to talk to after church. The King of Israel wants to command our entire attention.

KING OF KINGS

Who is the blessed and only Potentate,
the King of kings, and Lord of lords.
1 TIMOTHY 6:15 KJV

And he hath on his vesture and on his thigh a name written,
KING OF KINGS AND LORD OF LORDS.
REVELATION 19:16 KJV

To the mob of angry Jews awaiting his verdict, Pontius Pilate merely said, "Here is your king" (John 19:14). The Roman governor had questioned Jesus and found no fault in Him—but he had been intrigued by the notion of Jesus as king.

Although Pilate acquiesced to the crowd's demand that Jesus be crucified, he refused to be cowed completely by the religious leaders. Pilate's gesture was significant: Attached to Jesus' cross was a sign that read, "JESUS OF NAZARETH, THE KING OF THE JEWS." When the chief priests protested the wording, Pilate remained firm. "What I have written, I have written," he said (John 19:22).

For whatever reason he attached the sign—to rankle the religious Jews or to insert an ironic touch—little did Pilate realize the profound truth of his action. Yes, Jesus is the King of the Jews, but He is also the King of all kings.

To call someone a king in Bible times was to make a grand statement. Kings held supreme power over their subjects and were regarded with awe. They held the power of life and death and controlled the fate of thousands. The course of world history was affected by their decisions.

As the long-awaited Messiah or Christ, Jesus was recognized as the "Anointed One," the precursor to kingship. Writing to Timothy, Paul recognized Jesus' royal stature for all time: "Now to the King eternal, immortal, invisible, the only God, be honor and glory for ever and ever" (1 Timothy 1:17).

By defeating death and sin by His sacrifice on the cross, Jesus now reigns in heaven, awaiting the day when He will return to establish His new kingdom. At that time in the future, described by the apostle John, during the greatest confrontation in the history of the world, Jesus will defeat Satan, sending him to a fiery lake of burning sulfur. And on Jesus' robe and His thigh will not be Pilate's appellation but the name that belongs to Jesus and only Jesus: KING OF KINGS (Revelation 19:16).

Today, members of royal families are treated with equal parts respect and ridicule. It's hard to imagine falling on our faces in the presence of a modern-day king. Yet, one day, our King of kings will return to vanquish evil for all time—and to claim us as His. Awed by His majesty and glory, we will bow before Him. "Who is he, this King of glory?" David once asked rhetorically. In the next breath, he gives the answer: "The LORD Almighty—he is the King of glory" (Psalm 24:10).

LAMB OF GOD

The next day John saw Jesus coming toward him and said,
"Look, the Lamb of God, who takes away the sin of the world!"
JOHN 1:29

He had been born to prepare the way for Jesus' ministry on earth. And now, at last, John the Baptist was meeting Jesus face-to-face. In salutation, John addressed Jesus as the "Lamb of God," a role that was foretold in the first book of the Bible and ordained since the beginning of time.

When God asked Abraham to take Isaac, his beloved son, and sacrifice him on Moriah, God was painting a picture of the future sacrifice of His own Son, Jesus. Abraham himself said that God will provide the sacrifice (Genesis 22:8) and later named the site of the sacrifice of the ram "The Lord Will Provide."

But perhaps nowhere in the Bible is the parallel with Jesus' sacrifice seen more clearly than during the Israelites' final days in Egypt. When, after nine plagues sent by God, Pharaoh still refused to release the Israelites from bondage, God delivered the ultimate blow. The Israelites were instructed to slaughter one lamb per household. The lamb was to be without defect and they were to take some of its blood and put it on the sides and tops of their doorframes. The cooked lamb would then be consumed by each family as part of a feast known as the Lord's Passover. That night, all Egyptian families, whose houses did not have blood on the doors, suffered an incalculable loss: the death of all firstborn men and animals (see Exodus 12:12). For the Israelites, the years of bondage in Egypt were over.

Like the Passover lamb, Jesus is without defect or sin. And like that lamb's blood, Jesus' blood on the cross was shed to save God's people. As further confirmation of God's divine plan, the Passover feast—celebrated by Jesus and His disciples—occurred the night before Jesus was crucified.

During the Israelites' exodus toward the Promised Land, as part of God's laws for Israel, two lambs were to be slaughtered every day, one in the morning and one at twilight, on the altar in the Tent of Meeting and later, in the temple (see Exodus 29:38–41). When John addressed Jesus as the Lamb of God, religious Jews understood that He was being compared to the daily offerings. Not coincidentally, Jesus' death on the cross occurred around the time of the twilight sacrifice.

Lambs are known as submissive creatures, willing to be led. The same was true for Jesus, as described by the prophet Isaiah hundreds of years earlier: "He was led like a lamb to the slaughter, and as a sheep before her shearers is silent, so he did not open his mouth" (Isaiah 53:7). Jesus willingly laid down His life for the sins of humanity so that believers could have eternal life. Isaiah continued, "Yet it was the LORD's will to crush him and cause him to suffer, and though the LORD makes his life a guilt offering, he will see his offspring and prolong his days, and the will of the LORD will prosper in his hand" (Isaiah 53:10).

Jesus' sacrifice once and for all eliminated all other

sacrifices, which were unable to take away sin. Because of the precious blood of the Lamb of God, redemption is possible. Because of Jesus' resurrection, faith and hope are possible, too (see 1 Peter 1:18–21).

Peter admonished us to live our lives on earth "as strangers. . .in reverent fear" (1 Peter 1:17). Yet how often do we consider the price paid by Jesus for our salvation? We were saved not by a written contract, a hefty down payment, or a handshake, but by the spilled blood of the Lamb of God. Jesus gave His life for us.

LAST ADAM

So it is written: "The first man Adam became a living being";
the last Adam, a life-giving spirit.
1 CORINTHIANS 15:45

The story of the creation of Adam, the first man, is well known. He was created in the image of God by God and given dominion over all the earth. Initially, he was destined to live forever, at peace with God and the natural world. But soon Adam and the first woman, Eve, succumbed to temptation, defied God, and were banished by God from the Garden of Eden, a perfect place. Adam was "sentenced" to a life of hard work, a life that would one day end in death.

Like the first man, Jesus, who is called the Last Adam, was also created in the image of God. Yet Jesus, who existed before Adam and before the creation of the world, is called the firstborn (see Colossians 1:15) and He has dominion over not only the earth but heaven as well. And while He, like the first Adam, was tempted by Satan, Jesus overcame evil. Jesus, as God in the flesh, was fully human and fully divine, and as such, was incapable of sin. As the first Adam was a life-giver, beginning the human race, so the Last Adam gives life, eternal life, to those who trust in Him (see John 3:16).

Finally, the first Adam died because of his sin, but the Last Adam died to conquer sin—and then arose three days later to overcome death as well. As Paul wrote, "For if, by the trespass of the one man, death reigned through that one man, how much more will those who receive God's abundant provision of grace and of the gift of righteousness reign in life through the one man, Jesus Christ" (Romans 5:17).

It's hard to wrap your mind around the notion that all human beings, throughout all the centuries, are descended from one man. Yet, as believers, we're all children of God, too. Our past may be connected genetically to the first Adam, but our present and future is connected spiritually, physically, and emotionally to the Last Adam, our Savior, Jesus Christ.

LIGHT OF THE WORLD

Then spake Jesus again unto them, saying, I am the light
of the world: he that followeth me shall not walk
in darkness, but shall have the light of life.
JOHN 8:12 KJV

As long as I am in the world, I am the light of the world.
JOHN 9:5 KJV

In the Tent of Meeting, used during the journeys of Israel after they left Egypt, there was a magnificent golden lampstand. In the richly appointed temple built by King Solomon, there were ten candlesticks of gold. And in John's gospel, Jesus is probably standing in the courtyard of the temple rebuilt after the Babylonian captivity, where He declares Himself to be the light of the world.

Undoubtedly, the candles in the temple were glowing brilliantly, but their light dimmed beside Jesus. Much as the candles in the temple illuminated the table on which the showbread—a symbol of Jesus as the bread of life—was displayed, the glory of God shone on Jesus all the days He walked on earth.

The name "Light of the World" is used only three times in the New Testament—and all by Jesus. Jesus proclaimed Himself the source of life (and light) and all good things, a stance underscored by John: "In him was life; and the life was the light of men" (John 1:4 KJV). Jesus Himself said, "I am come a light into the world, that whosoever believeth on me should not abide in darkness" (John 12:46 KJV).

Jesus was also foretelling the future, a time when He would no longer be in the flesh with His disciples and others. After He had made His triumphal entry into Jerusalem, just days before His crucifixion, He said, "Yet a little while is the light with you. Walk while ye have the light, lest darkness come upon you: for he that walketh in darkness knoweth not whither he goeth" (John 12:35 KJV).

That darkness is considered the domain of Satan and the "rulers of the darkness of this world" (see Ephesians 6:12 KJV). As the light of the world, Jesus is the antithesis and antidote to such darkness.

Finally, Jesus said that His followers are the light of the world. "A city on a hill cannot be hidden," He said. To give light to everyone, His followers need to let their light "shine before men, that they may see your good deeds and praise your Father in heaven" (Matthew 5:14–16).

As you get to know a person, you often discover some interesting facts about their lives. Sometimes those tidbits are surprising. They may not look like former gymnasts or beauty queens, and some of the things you learn about their high school years would not make them ideal candidates to be teachers or doctors. Then consider yourself: Would people be surprised to learn that you are a Christian? When you let the goodness of God shine through your actions, no one will doubt the integrity of your faith.

LION OF THE TRIBE OF JUDAH

Then one of the elders said to me, "Do not weep!
See, the Lion of the tribe of Judah, the Root of David, has
triumphed. He is able to open the scroll and its seven seals."
REVELATION 5:5

The scroll the apostle John was describing is thought to be the "deed" to the earth. By opening the scroll and its seven seals, the Lion of Judah is unleashing the final assaults on the world before conquering sin and Satan and becoming the undisputed ruler.

The Lion of the tribe of Judah, the Root of David, is Jesus. A descendant of David (Matthew 1:1), Jesus could also trace His ancestry to Judah (Matthew 1:3; Luke 3:34), one of the twelve sons of Jacob. In a final blessing to his sons before he died, in which he foretold their future roles, Jacob said to Judah, "You are a lion's cub" (Genesis 49:9). That image of Jesus as the Lion was repeated by Amos, when he said, "The lion has roared—who will not fear? The Sovereign LORD has spoken—who can but prophesy?" (Amos 3:8).

While on earth, Jesus certainly offered glimpses of the Lion He is. He cleared the temple of money changers, calling His house "a house of prayer" (see Matthew 21:13); He also escaped an angry mob in His hometown of Nazareth that was determined to throw Him off a cliff (see Luke 4:28–30). Yet these previews pale in comparison with what is to come:

Jesus on a white horse, His eyes blazing like fire, the name "KING OF KINGS AND LORD OF LORDS" written on His robe (see Revelation 19:11–21).

Like a lion's roar, which can be heard for miles, Jesus' words have spread far and wide. As the Lion of the tribe of Judah, He continues to empower His followers to fearlessly go to the ends of the earth—and just around the corner, too. If you're lacking the courage to share your faith, remember you serve a Lion. Jesus will give you strength.

LORD OF HOSTS

And Elisha said, As the LORD of hosts liveth, before
whom I stand, surely, were it not that I regard the presence
of Jehoshaphat the king of Judah, I would not
look toward thee, nor see thee.

2 KINGS 3:14 KJV

Three kings had formed an unlikely alliance. Now marching
to battle against Moab, they were stopped in their tracks by a
common dilemma in their part of the world: no more water
for themselves or their animals. Desperate, they asked where
a prophet of the Lord might be, and they were directed to
Elisha. When the prophet saw King Jehoshaphat of Judah
among the group—the only righteous king of the three—he
agreed to inquire of the Lord for them.

Proclaiming the Lord of hosts, Elisha felt the hand of
the Lord come upon him—and then delivered the solution
to the kings' quandary. After digging ditches in the valley,
as the Lord directed, the kings' troops were rewarded the
next morning with a landscape filled with water. No rain had
fallen; water had simply flowed from the direction of Edom.
"This is an easy thing in the eyes of the LORD; he will also
hand Moab over to you," said the prophet (2 Kings 3:18).

The Lord of hosts, or Jehovah-sabaoth, is a name used
hundreds of times in the Old Testament. The name extols
God's sovereignty, His omnipotence, and His transcendence.
Familiar to many are the heavenly cries recorded by Isaiah:

"Holy, holy, holy, is the LORD of hosts: the whole earth is full of his glory" (Isaiah 6:3 KJV).

The word *sabaoth*, from the Hebrew *tsaba*, is used in connection with warfare and control of armies. Jehovah-sabaoth is thus interpreted as "Yahweh the warrior" or "Yahweh the divine king." Who else would David invoke when confronting the giant Goliath but the Lord of hosts? "Thou comest to me with a sword, and with a spear, and with a shield: but I come to thee in the name of the LORD of hosts, the God of the armies of Israel, whom thou hast defied" (1 Samuel 17:45 KJV).

But the Lord of hosts oversees more than mortal armies. He is also Lord over heavenly hosts, such as angels, and the host of heaven, or the physical stars in the sky, as well as the creator of the world. The psalmist says that God directs His angels to guard us (see Psalm 91:11), and in the Bible, angels were often the bearers of God's messages to men and women.

Perhaps the prophet Amos most eloquently described this name of the Lord: "For, lo, he that formeth the mountains, and createth the wind, and declareth unto man what is his thought, that maketh the morning darkness, and treadeth upon the high places of the earth, The LORD, The God of hosts, is his name" (Amos 4:13 KJV).

Time and again, we read in the Bible of battle lines drawn and armies facing off, with God directing the endgame for Israel or Judah. But what about the private battles we wage, the ones confined to the four walls of our lives? As believers, we're privileged to have God, the Lord of hosts, on our side.

Through the Holy Spirit, He can give us the words to say to assuage a heated or sticky situation. And when the time for words is over, He can nudge us to wrap our arms around a child, spouse, or friend and give us peace.

LORD OF LORDS

God, the blessed and only Ruler,
the King of kings and Lord of lords.
1 TIMOTHY 6:15

On his robe and on his thigh he has this name written:
KING OF KINGS AND LORD OF LORDS.
REVELATION 19:16

After the day of Pentecost, Jesus' disciples, who had been given the Holy Spirit as well as other spiritual gifts, began to preach, leading many to accept Jesus. As recorded by Luke in the book of Acts, these disciples then baptized new believers "into the name of the Lord Jesus" (see Acts 19:5). They acknowledged Jesus' sovereignty and power to save—and they knew Him as the Lord of lords.

The English word "Lord" had its roots in the original Hebrew Tetragrammaton *YHWH*, or Yahweh, which was then translated into the Greek *Kyrios*, meaning "power" or "powerful master." Jesus embodies such a description, as revealed in His words when He departed from His disciples:

"All authority in heaven and on earth has been given to me" (Matthew 28:18). When He died on the cross and was resurrected, overcoming death, He assumed lordship of both the dead and the living (see Romans 14:9).

There is one God and one Lord, or one Creator and omnipotent and omniscient ruler of the universe. All other gods and lords, those conceived of or given these earthly titles by mortal minds, are subservient to Lord Jesus. As Paul wrote, "Yet for us there is but one God, the Father, from whom all things came and for whom we live; and there is but one Lord, Jesus Christ, through whom all things came and through whom we live" (1 Corinthians 8:6).

Jesus wanted His disciples to know Him as Lord of lords, but He also wanted them to recognize His servant's heart. At the Last Supper, when Jesus began to wash the disciples' feet, Peter immediately objected, thinking it beneath his Lord. But Jesus said, "Now that I, your Lord and Teacher, have washed your feet, you also should wash one another's feet" (John 13:14). The lesson was well learned: Through their selfless lives and extraordinary commitment to Jesus, the disciples surely demonstrated that Jesus' lordship is one of power and love that knows no bounds.

The initials WWJD—"What would Jesus do?"—were seen everywhere for a while, most especially on plastic wristbands and other accessories. The gist of WWJD is really acknowledging Jesus' lordship, and denying the supremacy of other "gods." When we think about what Jesus would do, we're steered in the right direction, away from corrupting influences, and we're also led to worship and acknowledge Him as Savior and Lord.

MASTER

But be not ye called Rabbi: for one is your Master,
even Christ; and all ye are brethren.
MATTHEW 23:8 KJV

Once again, Jesus took on the Pharisees as examples of what not to do. Much to His disgust, these supposed religious men loved to sit in positions of honor, being feted by the masses of those less rigorously schooled than they. And they loved to have men call them "Rabbi." To Jesus, though, greatness comes by serving others, and not by having others serve you.

Before the fall of the second temple (AD 70), the title of Rabbi was one used for a respected teacher, a synonym for Master. The title *Rabboni*, used by Mary Magdalene when she saw Jesus alive after His crucifixion (see John 20:16), is an Aramaic word that means "my master."

As the Master, Jesus focused intently for three years on training the twelve men He selected as His disciples. They watched Him preach the message of salvation; they observed Him teaching by using parables. And as evidence of His divinity, they saw Him perform a myriad of miracles, including restoring life to His friend Lazarus. At the end of His ministry on earth, Jesus prayed, "As you sent me into the world, I have sent them into the world" (John 17:18).

While we can't sit at the knee of the Master as the disciples did, drinking in His words, we can open our Bibles and hear His voice. As Paul wrote, "All Scripture is God-breathed and is useful for teaching" (2 Timothy 3:16). We don't have to be in His "classroom" because we have Jesus' "lectures" right in God's Word. All we have to do is read—and believe.

MEDIATOR

For there is one God and one mediator between
God and men, the man Christ Jesus.
1 TIMOTHY 2:5

Before Jesus came on the scene, the high priest in the temple had the role of mediator. Once a year, the high priest entered the Holy of Holies to make an animal sacrifice for the atonement of the sins of Israel (see Leviticus 16). Since Jesus' death on the cross and resurrection, which served as the atonement for our sins, such a ritual is no longer necessary. God has "reconciled" the world to Himself through Jesus (see 2 Corinthians 5:19). Jesus is now our Mediator.

From a legal standpoint, a mediator is a go-between, someone who stands between two parties in a dispute to reach a common goal. In his or her role, the mediator must have a complete understanding of both parties and their wishes and the nature of the dispute itself.

From a spiritual standpoint, the two parties, God and humanity, are separated by sin. The common goal is salvation, because God wants everyone to believe in Him. To achieve that goal, we must ask Jesus to forgive our wrongdoings and we must accept Jesus as Lord and Savior.

Jesus, fully man and fully divine, understands the human condition. As the author of Hebrews wrote: "We do not have a high priest who is unable to sympathize with our weaknesses, but we have one who has been tempted in every way, just as we are—yet was without sin" (Hebrews 4:15). Jesus is also aware of the human craving for peace. As "our peace," Jesus has destroyed the barrier that separated men and women from God (see Ephesians 2:14–16).

Jesus, who is superior to the high priests of old, is the only one qualified to be Mediator. As He said, "I am the way and the truth and the life. No one comes to the Father except through me" (John 14:6).

How many people know the real you? We all have our long-hidden secrets and most of us allow precious few, if any, to know them. To Jesus, our Mediator, our lives are an open book. He knows the hurt that won't go away, the love we can't profess, the guilt that still consumes us—and the sin we don't confess. When we accept Him as Savior, He immediately becomes our go-between to the Father, ready to defend us, ready to plead our case, ready to love us.

MESSIAH

He first found his own brother Simon, and said to him, "We have found the Messiah" (which is translated, the Christ).
JOHN 1:41 NKJV

Andrew and most probably John, the writer of this gospel account, were initially followers of John the Baptist. But John the Baptist's role was to point the way to Jesus by telling people about Jesus, baptizing Jesus, and then directing his own disciples to seek Jesus themselves.

After spending just one day with Jesus, Andrew couldn't wait to tell his brother Simon Peter the most remarkable news. He, a common fisherman, had found the long-awaited Messiah! In short order, Simon, soon to be known simply as Peter, became one of Jesus' disciples himself.

Andrew's announcement of the Messiah, or "Anointed One," was the climax of thousands of years of waiting and hundreds of Old Testament prophecies. To his son Judah, the patriarch Jacob had declared, "The scepter shall not depart from Judah, nor a lawgiver from between his feet, until Shiloh comes; and to Him shall be the obedience of the people" (Genesis 49:10 NKJV). Shiloh, which means "The Peaceful One," was another name for the Messiah. Such a prophecy had to be fulfilled before AD 70 when Jerusalem and much of Judah were destroyed by Rome.

Many prophecies of the Messiah concern His relationship to David. As God told David, "I will set up your seed after you, who will come from your body, and I will establish his kingdom. He shall build a house for My name, and I will establish the throne of his kingdom forever. I will be his Father, and he shall be My son" (2 Samuel 7:12–14 NKJV). Jesus' mother, Mary, was a direct descendant of David, as was His stepfather Joseph.

The prophet Daniel foretold not only the arrival of the Messiah but also His death and the subsequent destruction of Jerusalem. Daniel was divinely inspired to predict that sixty-nine "Sabbaths" (or 483 sabbatical years) would pass between the decree to rebuild Jerusalem after the Babylonian captivity and the arrival of the Anointed One (see Daniel 9:24–27).

To Moses, God said that He would "raise up" a prophet like him, from among his own brothers (see Deuteronomy 18:15). While many religious Jews believed that God was speaking of Joshua, who led the Israelites into the Promised Land, two prominent early Christians were directed by God to believe otherwise. Shortly before he was stoned to death, the apostle Stephen quoted this scripture (see Acts 7:37), as did Peter while he was preaching at the temple (see Acts 3:22). Peter was trying to convince the Jews that this long-awaited Messiah, Jesus, had come to preach to them first—but sadly, they had rejected Him.

Still, the spark igniting the Christian faith had been lit among a small group of Jewish men, the disciples, who would testify far and wide that they had seen the Messiah.

Do you remember when you first accepted Jesus as Savior? Likely, you couldn't wait to tell someone close to you what had happened—just like Andrew. Andrew didn't need to find confirmation in the scriptures and he didn't need to consult with the religious leaders in the temple. He simply felt the truth of the Messiah in his heart. Finding Jesus isn't a laborious process. . .it's a beautiful step of faith.

MIGHTY GOD

For to us a child is born, to us a son is given. . . .
And he will be called. . .Mighty God.
ISAIAH 9:6

The prophet Isaiah was really going out on a limb: Whoever heard of a baby being called the Mighty God? But such a statement wasn't coming from the prophet's imagination. Isaiah had been given this message from God. And it was God who was coming to earth, in the flesh, Emmanuel (God with us), to establish His kingdom "with justice and righteousness from that time on and forever" (Isaiah 9:7).

Jesus was heralded as the Mighty God, the Hebrew *El Gibbor*, at His birth. Witness the angels proclaiming to the shepherds that their Savior, who was Christ the Lord, had been born (see Luke 2:8–12). Witness the Magi inquiring in Jerusalem where the one "who has been born king of the Jews" might be found (see Matthew 2:2), and upon finding Him, bowing down and worshiping Him.

At the age of twelve, Jesus stunned the learned men in Jerusalem's temple with His uncanny command of scripture.

Because He was without sin, as a grown man, He resisted Satan's offers of power and grandeur and began His humble ministry on earth. His might, while reflected in numerous miracles, was most clearly demonstrated on the cross and beyond. For hours, He endured the shame and pain of the cross—and then arose from the tomb three days later, the wounds still visible but His flesh uncorrupted. Only the Mighty God could overcome the grave and then ascend forty days later to sit at the right hand of God the Father in heaven.

Jesus, Mighty God, was given power over creation (see John 1:3) and heaven, with "angels, authorities and powers in submission to him" (1 Peter 3:22). One day, when He returns to earth, His might will be displayed for all to see. The prophet Daniel described seeing the Son of man, or Jesus, "coming with the clouds of heaven." His dominion, Daniel wrote, "will not pass away, and his kingdom is one that will never be destroyed" (Daniel 7:13–14).

Do you prefer giving gifts or receiving them? Many people have trouble being on the receiving end. They're uncomfortable being acknowledged or they're hard to buy for, or they're afraid they'll respond inappropriately to the gift. If you're like this, here's something that will change your mind: As Isaiah wrote, Jesus, the Mighty God, is a gift to us. He satisfies the needs of everyone—and He keeps on giving until you respond to Him.

MORNING STAR

I am the root and the offspring of David,
and the bright and morning star.

REVELATION 22:16 KJV

John had been given an amazing vision of events to come—startling, jaw-dropping, awe-inspiring occurrences—and now he fell to the ground at the feet of an angel. Immediately, though, the angel admonished him, "Worship God!" (see Revelation 22:8–9). And as the apostle did so, Jesus spoke again, departing words, words that filled John with hope.

Jesus calls Himself the Morning Star, the beacon heralding the end of the night. He is the light of salvation to all who call upon His name, "the sun of righteousness. . .with healing in its wings" (Malachi 4:2). He is a bright star of great beauty, "the radiance of God's glory and the exact representation of his being" (Hebrews 1:3). Much as the morning star remains the same, guiding sailors and seekers, Jesus told His followers that He would be with them always, "to the very end of the age" (Matthew 28:20). As Jesus said, "I have come into the world as a light, so that no one who believes in me should stay in darkness" (John 12:46).

The current events in the Middle East have led many Bible scholars to speculate that John's vision may be about to unfold in real time. While such discussions can be upsetting, as believers we have nothing to fear. Our salvation is secure, and our hope is placed on that great dawning day when Jesus, our Morning Star, vanquishes darkness once and for all.

And he came and dwelt in a city called Nazareth:
that it might be fulfilled which was spoken by the
prophets, He shall be called a Nazarene.

MATTHEW 2:23 KJV

To escape the murderous rampage of King Herod, who had ordered all baby boys two years and younger to be killed, Joseph and Mary had fled to Egypt with Jesus. Now that Herod was dead, Joseph returned to Israel, but he had his qualms about settling in Judea. Instead, he took his family to the district of Galilee, and to the town of Nazareth. Jesus would thus be called a Nazarene, a name meaning a resident of the vicinity of Nazareth.

Although no Old Testament prophets foretold that Jesus would be raised in Nazareth, the one most cited, Isaiah, referred to Jesus as the Branch, which in Hebrew is *nacar* or *necer*, a word similar to Nazarene (see Isaiah 11:1). In general, Nazarenes were a despised people, perhaps because of the region's history of pagan influences. Recall Jesus' disciple Nathanael's comment—"Nazareth! Can anything good come from there?" (John 1:46). Accordingly, Isaiah alluded to Jesus as despised and rejected (see Isaiah 53:3) and David foretold "a worm and not a man, scorned by men and despised by the people" (Psalm 22:6).

Dealing with rejection is one of the hardest life lessons to learn. Yet as the Nazarene, Jesus suffered rejection early and often, even being rejected by His fellow Nazarenes when He began His ministry. And that was only the beginning—Calvary's cross awaited Him. When you're rejected, and dejected, remember the Nazarene and pour out your heart to Him.

PASSOVER LAMB

Get rid of the old yeast that you may be a new
batch without yeast—as you really are. For Christ,
our Passover lamb, has been sacrificed.
1 CORINTHIANS 5:7

Ever since the Israelites were delivered out of Egypt by God, Jewish people have celebrated the yearly Passover feast. In ancient times, the feast consisted of bitter herbs, unleavened bread, and lamb. The herbs represented repentance and confession of sin; the unleavened bread was a symbol of purity; and the lamb was to remember the blood sacrifices of the first Passover and God's deliverance of His people from Pharaoh.

God gave the Israelites particular instructions as to the Passover lamb: The animal had to be a male lamb without defect, roasted whole with none of its bones broken. No meat was to be left until the following morning (see Numbers 9:1–14).

When Jesus celebrated His last Passover on earth with His disciples, just hours before He would be betrayed, arrested, and crucified, He described Himself as the feast. After He gave thanks for the bread, Jesus said, "Take and eat; this is my body." And after He gave thanks for the wine, He said, "This is my blood of the covenant, which is poured out for many for the forgiveness of sins" (see Matthew 26:26–28).

Jesus is the Passover Lamb: He was a sinless man who was killed on the cross (or roasted over the fire), a sacrifice that was made without any of His bones being broken (see John 19:33). Before the following morning, His body was removed from the cross and placed in the tomb.

The covenant Jesus spoke of, the one in which God's law would be in the minds of the people, written on their hearts (see Jeremiah 31:33), would be fulfilled by His sacrifice on the cross. As the Passover Lamb, His blood was the ultimate atonement for sin, a one-time sacrifice negating the ritual temple sacrifices. As Peter wrote, we were redeemed "from the empty way of life handed down to you from your forefathers. . .with the precious blood of Christ, a lamb without blemish or defect" (1 Peter 1:18–19).

Baker's yeast, a type of fermented fungi used in baking, was as essential in ancient Egypt as it is today. When the Israelites hurriedly pulled up stakes in Egypt, though, they had no time to produce yeast and had to bake unleavened bread. As part of God's plan, they were symbolically leaving behind the old on their journey to the new. When we ask Jesus into our hearts, we need to do the same. Whatever may lead us back to a sinful lifestyle or bad habits we need to avoid, discard, or leave behind.

PHYSICIAN

*But when Jesus heard that, he said unto them, They that be
whole need not a physician, but they that are sick.*
MATTHEW 9:12 KJV

Jesus was having dinner with a new disciple—but once
again, He was being critically observed by the Pharisees.
The Pharisees, who were not invited to dine with Jesus,
nonetheless made sure He could hear what they were saying.
"Why does your teacher eat with tax collectors and 'sinners'?"
they asked the other disciples (verse 11).

Jesus the Physician came to heal sinners, and to give men
and women the opportunity for life after death. He healed
many who had physical ailments or disabilities, and the Bible
only describes a fraction of those healed by His touch, His
words, or His actions. A woman who had been bleeding for
years merely had to touch His cloak (see Mark 5:25–34); a
Roman centurion returned home to find his servant healed by
Jesus' command (see Matthew 8:5–13); and Jairus' daughter
was restored to life when Jesus took her hand (see Mark
5:35–43).

Many of us dread going to the doctor. We rationalize that
we know as much as the doctor or that we'll be back on our
feet in no time. Those excuses don't work when the diagnosis
is sin and the physician is Jesus. As sinners, we are all destined
to die one day (see Romans 6:23). But when we believe in
Jesus, after we die we *will* live again, with Him in heaven.

POTENTATE

Which in his times he shall shew, who is the blessed and only Potentate, the King of kings, and Lord of lords.
I TIMOTHY 6:15 KJV

The apostle Paul knew that his days were numbered. It was only a matter of time before Emperor Nero would set about to eliminate the "scourge" of Christianity from the Roman Empire—and execute one of its leading proponents, the fearless Paul. So Paul put pen to paper, or quill to papyrus, and wrote to his beloved protégé, the young minister Timothy. Above all, he wanted Timothy to "fight the good fight of the faith" (I Timothy 6:12) because he served a true Potentate.

Jesus is the blessed and only Potentate, from the Latin *potens*, meaning "powerful," by definition a ruler who is above the law.

When He came to earth, He was born under the Mosaic law and grew up abiding by its severe regulations. Yet He came to abolish the law and to redeem those who were under the law (see Galatians 4:4–5). As Paul wrote, "Christ is the end of the law so that there may be righteousness for everyone who believes" (Romans 10:4). Because Jesus sacrificed Himself on the cross, we are saved by His blood—not by slavish compliance with the law.

All Americans are governed by federal, state, and municipal statutes. Yet the complexity of our justice system pales when compared to the Mosaic code. Imagine not wearing clothes made of two different kinds of material or not planting two different kinds of seeds in your garden (see Leviticus 19:19)! Praise God, we serve a Potentate who is above the law, who has saved us by His grace.

PRINCE OF PEACE

*For unto us a child is born, unto us a son is given. . .
and his name shall be called. . .The Prince of Peace.*
ISAIAH 9:6 KJV

For hundreds of years, Isaiah's words had rung out from synagogues and been passed from parent to child in hopeful expectation. In the first century AD, though, the scripture had taken on particular importance. Since AD 6, the province of Judea had been under Roman occupation—which meant a constant military presence even in Jerusalem's outer temple court, plus heavy taxation. If the Prince of Peace came, He would surely rescue His people from such tyranny!

Jesus the Prince of Peace did come, but, to the consternation of many, the peace He brought did not vanquish Rome. Instead He brought *shalom*, the Hebrew word for "peace," which has been translated "completeness" and "contentment." Jesus' sacrifice would signal the beginning of the new covenant, *completing* Jeremiah's prophecy (see Jeremiah 31:33). Those who accept Him as Savior are rewarded with *contentment* of the soul and peace with God through the new covenant relationship.

Before the advent of the Prince of Peace, peace with God meant obeying His commands. As God told Isaiah, "If only you had paid attention to my commands, your peace would have been like a river, your righteousness like the waves of the sea" (Isaiah 48:18). When the people trusted in Him, they would realize God's plans to prosper them, plans to give them hope and a future (see Jeremiah 29:11).

Jesus' mission of peace was heralded by angels, who proclaimed to the shepherds in Bethlehem's fields, "Glory to God in the highest, and on earth peace to men on whom his favor rests" (Luke 2:14). For His disciples, Jesus calmed the sea (see Matthew 8:23–27); for all people for all time, Jesus overcame the world (see John 16:33).

As the prophesied arbiter of peace, Jesus declared Himself openly and on several occasions. "Peace I leave with you; my peace I give you," He said. "I do not give to you as the world gives. Do not let your hearts be troubled and do not be afraid" (John 14:27).

Waiting is hard to do, and it's especially trying to wait for something wonderful. A child can't wait to open gifts on Christmas, a bride and groom can't wait to take their wedding vows, and an expectant couple (and yes, those future grandparents) can't wait to hold their baby in their arms. Just like those early Judeans, we're also waiting for something wonderful—for Jesus, the Prince of Peace, to come. When He returns the second time, He will usher in His eternal kingdom, a kingdom of shalom.

PROPITIATION

And he is the propitiation for our sins: and not for ours only,
but also for the sins of the whole world.

1 JOHN 2:2 KJV

Every year on the Day of Atonement, the high priest would enter the Most Holy Place, the holiest place of the tabernacle or temple, and sprinkle blood on the mercy seat. The mercy seat was the gold-covered lid of the ark of the covenant, the sacred vessel that held the golden pot of manna and the tablets on which the Ten Commandments were written. When the priest did this, he was offering a *propitiation*, or an appeasement, for the sins of the people. In other words, he was making peace with God.

Such an offering of blood was required every year because men and women are habitually sinful (see Romans 3:23) and no one offering made by a mortal high priest was capable of satisfying God's sense of justice because God is completely holy.

So God in His infinite wisdom provided His own solution: He sent His only Son, Jesus, to spill His blood and die on the cross. Jesus became the propitiation for the sins of humanity for all time, and in so doing, reconciled humankind to God. As John the Baptist declared, "Look, the Lamb of God, who takes away the sin of the world!" (John 1:29).

Some of us always see things in terms of "black and white," while others tend to consider "gray" areas. In terms of our salvation, though, there is only one way of looking at it, one way of achieving it—and that is through Jesus. "I am the way and the truth and the life. No one comes to the Father except through me," He said (John 14:6). Only Jesus, as the propitiation for our sins, could save us by His blood and lead us to the Father in heaven.

RABBI

Nathanael answered and saith unto him, Rabbi,
thou art the Son of God; thou art the King of Israel.
JOHN 1:49 KJV

What had happened to turn this skeptic into a believer? Moments earlier, Nathanael had mocked Jesus' hometown. But that was before Jesus declared what He knew about His future disciple. Amazed, Nathanael acknowledged that he was in the presence of not only a great teacher but the Messiah.

Jesus was accorded the title of Rabbi by many, including common people and religious leaders. It is a name that means "teacher," "great one," and "my master." In the early first century, "Rabbi" was more a title of respect than an occupation, though rabbis were learned men familiar with the ancient scriptures.

As Rabbi, Jesus traveled from town to town, visiting synagogues and reading from scripture. He taught using parables, or stories incorporating scenes from daily life, a familiar technique employed by other first-century teachers. But clearly, Jesus was no ordinary teacher. Following one particular sermon, Matthew recorded, "the people were astonished at his doctrine: For he taught them as one having authority" (Matthew 7:28–29 KJV). As Nathanael declared, the Rabbi Jesus was also the Son of God.

The exchange between Nathanael and Jesus was brief but telling. In two sentences, Jesus conveyed to Nathanael a simple truth: *I know you.* Jesus didn't give His life to save strangers but to save those He knows and loves.

RANSOM

Who gave himself a ransom for all,
to be testified in due time.
1 TIMOTHY 2:6 KJV

The prophet Hosea foretold the result of Jesus as Ransom: "I will ransom them from the power of the grave; I will redeem them from death" (Hosea 13:14). Indeed, Jesus' sacrifice of Himself on the cross freed those who believe in Him from eternal damnation.

In the New Testament the word "ransom" comes from the Greek *lutron*, signifying a payment made to liberate captives or slaves. Because "everyone who sins is a slave to sin" (John 8:34), Jesus acted as our ransom, "paying" for our freedom with His life, a payment made by the shedding of His blood.

But the sacrifice of Jesus is something more: His ransom is an act of love. As Paul wrote, "But God demonstrates his own love for us in this: While we were still sinners, Christ died for us" (Romans 5:8). By Jesus' wounds—His pierced hands and feet—we have been healed of sin and given new life (see 1 Peter 2:24).

Although we prize our freedoms and are quick to decry oppressive regimes, we ourselves were slaves to sin before we accepted His gift of salvation. Even after salvation, we can allow sin to have power over us. It's easy to see how one compromise leads to another, or how moral precedents collapse under the weight of peer pressure, greed, or lust (or name your poison). Praise God that Jesus was our Ransom, and that in Him is forgiveness and a future.

REDEEMER

Fear not, thou worm Jacob, and ye men of Israel; I will help thee, saith the LORD, and thy redeemer, the Holy One of Israel.
ISAIAH 41:14 KJV

To the ancients, the idea of a redeemer coming to the aid of Israel was a familiar one. Such a person was known as a kinsman-redeemer, and his role was well established in Mosaic law.

In the book of Ruth, the destitute Naomi, a widow, discovered that Boaz, a wealthy landowner, was a close relative of her dead husband and a kinsman-redeemer. As such, he was able to marry Naomi's widowed daughter-in-law Ruth, thereby redeeming them both from a life of poverty. Kinsman-redeemers could also purchase relatives who had been sold into slavery (see Leviticus 25:47–49). The redeemer had to be a kinsman who was able and willing to pay the price.

As our Redeemer, Jesus satisfies those requirements of old. By becoming part of the human race, He became our kinsman, but one who is without sin. From the beginning of time, it was God's plan that Jesus would come to earth to offer Himself as the redeeming sacrifice for our sins. Jesus thus willingly and ably redeemed humankind from a life of slavery to sin.

Why do we need redemption? Plain and simple, because we sin. Thus, our redemption by Jesus was supremely an act of mercy. As Paul wrote, "For God has bound all men over to disobedience so that he may have mercy on them all" (Romans 11:32). Without redemption, humankind would be condemned to hell—that would be the only recourse for a disobedient life. Because Jesus is the Redeemer, there is the possibility of forgiveness for sin. And because Jesus is the Redeemer, there is the possibility of life after physical death if one professes faith in Him.

To forgive and forget is a nice platitude that is harder to do than it sounds. If we feel we've been wronged by the same person time and again, that laundry list of bad deeds seems to resurface without prompting. Thankfully, God is not like us. Because Jesus is our Redeemer, we can go directly to the Father for forgiveness—and He *will* forgive and forget. "I, even I, am he who blots out your transgressions, for my own sake, and remembers your sins no more" (Isaiah 43:25).

REFINER

But who can endure the day of his coming?
Who can stand when he appears?
For he will be like a refiner's fire.
MALACHI 3:2

To Malachi, God gave a prophecy of two messengers. The first, whom God said, "will prepare the way before me" (3:1), is understood to be John the Baptist, who declared those same intentions himself (see John 1:23). The second, God said, was "the messenger of the covenant, whom you desire" (3:1). That messenger, who has been called the Refiner, can only be Jesus. He was sent by God to establish a new covenant of grace, which was accomplished by His sacrifice on the cross.

When we ask Jesus into our hearts, we also desire to be like Him. To that end, Jesus, the Refiner, purifies our souls much like metals were purified in ancient times. In those days, silver and gold were melted down in the refiner's fire, a process that separated the impurities from the metals, leaving the gold and silver intact.

Likewise, when we are tested by Jesus, though the process may be painful, the result will be a more joyful life (see James 1:2–4). We will be able to "stand when he appears"—a reference to the final judgment (see Revelation 20:11–15)—because we belong to Him.

No one relishes the bad times. But if we think of them as opportunities to develop perseverance, as James did, there's reason for hope. When a new day dawns, and it will by God's perfect timing, you will like what you see in the mirror: someone mature and complete, someone refined by Jesus.

REFUGE

You have been a refuge for the poor,
a refuge for the needy in his distress.
ISAIAH 25:4

Much like Noah's ark was the only place of refuge to survive the great flood, and much like the cities of refuge of the Old Testament were the only places to escape punishment and death, Jesus is our refuge.

Because Noah "found favor in the eyes of the LORD" (Genesis 6:8), he and his family, and the pairs of all creatures, were offered refuge in the ark—but all others perished. When Joshua and the people of Israel settled into the land, they were to establish cities of refuge to protect those who killed unintentionally and without malice from the "avengers of blood" (see Joshua 20:1–6). Such cities offered easy access, provided sustenance to the escapees, and were open to all who needed protection.

When we ask Jesus to be our Savior, we find favor in His eyes and He becomes our refuge. Only Jesus can save us from eternal death; there is no other way to salvation (see Acts 4:12). And once we are His, we are saved from the clutches of that perennial avenger of blood known as Satan. Jesus will never turn away anyone who comes to Him (see John 6:37).

When the sky gets dark and the wind picks up, that's the time to seek shelter from the elements. Likewise, when problems begin to multiply and you can't see a way out, turn to Jesus as your Refuge. "Come to me," Jesus said, "all you who are weary and burdened, and I will give you rest" (Matthew 11:28).

THE RESURRECTION AND THE LIFE

Jesus said unto her, I am the resurrection, and the life: he that believeth in me, though he were dead, yet shall he live.

JOHN 11:25 KJV

In the Gospel accounts, Jesus was depicted as the son of Mary and Joseph; the teacher and mentor of the twelve disciples; and the Son of God. But He was also described as a friend to Lazarus and his sisters, Martha and Mary. Curiously, though, in John 11, when word reached Jesus that Lazarus was sick, Jesus did nothing. In fact, He stayed where He was for two more days before traveling with His disciples to Lazarus' home in Bethany.

When Jesus arrived, Lazarus was dead and had been buried for four days. Confronting Him, Martha and Mary had one big question practically written on their faces: "Where *were* You?" If He had been there, they knew He would have saved their brother. They knew that because they believed that Jesus was the Son of God and because He had already healed many.

Instead of answering Martha directly, Jesus told her He was the Resurrection and the Life. Instead of offering His friend's grieving sister comfort, Jesus offered eternal hope.

And then, guided by Mary, He went to the tomb and wept. Moments later, after praying to God the Father, Jesus commanded Lazarus to walk out of the tomb. Suddenly

Lazarus appeared, his body still shrouded in the linen burial garments.

Before He and the disciples returned to Bethany, Jesus foretold what would happen. He said that the purpose of Lazarus' sickness, which wouldn't end in death, was to glorify God's Son (see verse 4). By bringing Lazarus back from the dead, Jesus was showing Himself as the Resurrection. By Lazarus's faith, and that of his sisters, Jesus was showing that He is Life. Whoever believes in Jesus will never die; eternal life is a reality.

Lazarus' death and resurrection was also foreshadowing the events about to unfold in Jesus' life. Very soon, Jesus would be handed over to the Jewish and Roman authorities to be crucified on a wooden cross and then buried in a tomb sealed with a giant stone and guarded by Roman soldiers. At Lazarus' tomb, Jesus had demonstrated He already had power over death. When He arose from the dead after three days in His own tomb, He underscored His power for all time. "Death has been swallowed up in victory," Paul wrote (1 Corinthians 15:54). Because Jesus is the Resurrection and the Life, all Christians can claim victory as well.

Like Martha and Mary, at times we all question Jesus. We may not have lost someone we love, but we wonder why things turned out the way they did. And "wonder" may be putting it gently: We cry, stomp our feet, wring our hands, and lose sleep. When we've had our say, it's best to consider Martha's reaction. No matter what happened or why, she said, "I believe that you are the Christ, the Son of God" (verse 27). Jesus, the Resurrection and the Life, came to earth and died for us so that we might have life with Him. One day we'll have answers to our questions, but for the moment, we need to keep strong in the faith.

RIGHTEOUSNESS

In his days Judah shall be saved, and Israel shall dwell safely: and this is his name whereby he shall be called,
THE LORD OUR RIGHTEOUSNESS.
JEREMIAH 23:6 KJV

The prophet Jeremiah wrote and spoke out during the reigns of the last five kings of Judah—before Jerusalem would be conquered by Babylon in 586 BC. Despite what was about to happen to Judah, God had not forgotten His people. One day God would "raise up to David a righteous Branch" (verse 5), a king who would be called our Righteousness; His Son, Jesus.

Paul wrote that Jesus is our righteousness, holiness, and redemption (see 1 Corinthians 1:30). As sinners, we need the righteousness of Jesus in order to be saved. By God's grace we have been acquitted for Jesus' sake (because of His death on the cross and resurrection) to receive the free gift of salvation—if we but believe. Once we profess belief, we, too, become righteous in the eyes of God and are thus entitled to the reward of righteousness, which is eternal life.

Yes, once we are His, we are His forever. King Solomon wrote that "the righteous cannot be uprooted" (Proverbs 12:3).

He goes on to say that "the root of the righteous flourishes" (Proverbs 12:12). That's because the "root" is Jesus.

Eventually most people like to "put down roots" somewhere. Usually such longings occur when you get a "real" job or get married or can't think about packing one more time. God wants your faith to develop deep roots in Him, too. When our faith grows and flourishes, our Righteousness touches others.

ROCK

He is the Rock, his works are perfect,
and all his ways are just.

DEUTERONOMY 32:4

In a song to the Israelites shortly before he died, Moses gave his people a brief history lesson. His song reminded them that throughout all the generations, though the people had turned to other gods, their Rock had not forsaken them. Their Rock was a Savior; He was not like any other gods.

Recalling the Israelites' exodus from Egypt to the Promised Land, Paul wrote, "They all ate the same spiritual food and drank the same spiritual drink; for they drank from the spiritual rock that accompanied them, and that rock was Christ" (1 Corinthians 10:3–4). Jesus, who is the same yesterday and today, and who has been since before the beginning of time, is the Rock.

As the spiritual rock of the Christian faith, Jesus is the foundation and chief cornerstone of His church (see 1 Corinthians 3:11 and Ephesians 2:19–22). There have been and will be many "rocks" embedded in its structure, but there is only one Head, and that is Jesus. As David wrote, "And who is the Rock except our God?" (Psalm 18:31).

One of the greatest blessings is to have been raised in a Christian home. What a thrill to hold a family Bible and know that previous generations have read and cherished God's Word! If that doesn't describe your family, imagine the legacy *you* can leave. How has Jesus been your Rock?

ROOT OF DAVID

I am the root and the offspring of David,
and the bright and morning star.
REVELATION 22:16 KJV

Many prophecies speak of the Messiah being the descendant of King David—and two genealogies in the New Testament provide the necessary evidence. But as John records, Jesus acknowledged Himself as the Root of David, too. How can Jesus be the root *and* the offspring of the legendary king? To use Jesus' own names, how can the Branch be the Root?

The genealogies again supply the answers. Matthew's genealogy traces Jesus' lineage from the patriarch Abraham to His stepfather Joseph (see Matthew 1:1–16). From this record, Jesus can clearly be seen as the offspring of David. Luke's record (see Luke 3:23–37), however, gives a different result. Luke traces Jesus' ancestry from Mary's father, Heli, all the way back to Adam, who was "the son of God." Because Jesus is acknowledged as the Creator—"all things were created by him and for him" (Colossians 1:16)—Jesus must also be the Root of David. Paul continues by stating, "He is before all things, and in him all things hold together" (Colossians 1:17).

Some pictures defy description. Consider an ocean beach at sunrise; springtime in an alpine meadow; evergreen trees blanketed in snow; pristine, undulating sand dunes. Such beauty, like its Creator, is beyond comprehension. Jesus, the Root of David, is too wonderful for words.

ROSE OF SHARON

I am the rose of Sharon, and the lily of the valleys.
SONG OF SOLOMON 2:1 KJV

Because the Song of Solomon is a wedding song, many Bible scholars have interpreted the book as an allegory about the Bridegroom Jesus' love for His church. However one wishes to read the book, as an allegory or as simply a dialogue of love between King Solomon and his bride, the image of Jesus as the rose of Sharon is vivid and real.

At the time of Solomon, Sharon was a vast plain, extending from the Mediterranean Sea to the hill country west of Jerusalem, and was known for its beautiful flowers. To compare Jesus to a rose is to say that He is the most beautiful flower, a bloom without imperfection. As a plain or meadow is a serene place, so to be with Jesus is to be at peace. As David wrote, "The LORD is my shepherd, I shall not be in want. He makes me lie down in green pastures" (Psalm 23:1–2).

If it's been one of those days, all you want is a moment's peace. But if you manage this feat, you still have to face the music sometime. Jesus, the Rose of Sharon, gives a different kind of peace—the kind that lasts, if we truly trust in Him. "Do not let your hearts be troubled and do not be afraid," He said (John 14:27).

SACRIFICE

Live a life of love, just as Christ loved us and gave himself up
for us as a fragrant offering and sacrifice to God.
EPHESIANS 5:2

At the moment of Jesus' death, the curtain separating the Most Holy Place from the Holy Place in Jerusalem's temple was torn in two, from top to bottom (see Matthew 27:51). That act was symbolic evidence that the necessary sacrifice had been made. No longer would the high priest have to enter the Most Holy Place once a year and make atonement for sin. No longer would any blood sacrifice have to be made.

By His sacrifice, Jesus brought down all barriers separating man and God. Only Jesus was worthy to be the single sacrifice for all time for all human beings.

Like the spotless, flawless lambs offered as sacrifices, Jesus was without blemish or sin because He is holy. As the writer of Hebrews penned, "You have loved righteousness and hated wickedness; therefore God, your God, has set you above your companions by anointing you with the oil of joy" (Hebrews 1:9). But because it was impossible for the blood of animals to take away sin, Jesus became incarnate, being born on earth, with the sole purpose of being that sacrifice and thereby offering salvation to all who believe in Him (see Hebrews 9:26–28).

Guilt is one of the evil one's favorite tools. Satan knows just how to make us feel worthless and unworthy of receiving forgiveness. But no one is beyond the saving grasp of Jesus—and no one was left out of the saving grace of His sacrifice. Jesus died for you!

SAVIOR

The LORD lives! Praise be to my Rock!
Exalted be God, the Rock, my Savior!
2 SAMUEL 22:47

My soul glorifies the Lord and my
spirit rejoices in God my Savior.
LUKE 1:46–47

Mary already knew something exceedingly special had happened to her. After all, how many teenaged girls in Galilee were visited by angels? And not only that. . .how many teenaged girls in Galilee had been chosen by God to be the mother of His Son? But when she went to visit her relative Elizabeth, who was also expecting a baby, Mary must have been astounded at Elizabeth's welcome. Filled by the Holy Spirit, Elizabeth exclaimed, "Blessed are you among women!" And then she said, "Blessed is she who has believed that what the Lord has said to her will be accomplished!" (see Luke 1:39–45).

Mary is to be commended. Instead of expressing doubt or asking questions of the angel, Mary accepted her situation dutifully—and with reverent awe. Further, she acknowledged God as her Savior.

The son Mary would bear would be named Jesus, which is from the Hebrew *Yehoshua*, meaning "Jehovah saves." That name and its meaning would become the foundation of Christianity. Only Jesus could be the Savior; only Jesus could save us from our sins. As Luke wrote, "Salvation is found in no one else, for there is no other name under heaven given to men by which we must be saved" (Acts 4:12).

As Savior, Jesus has counted all believers as righteous— even though they are sinners—in a process known as justification. He did this by His sacrifice on the cross and the shedding of His blood.

As Savior, Jesus has made all believers holy, a process known as sanctification. He has done this by His sacrifice on the cross and the shedding of His blood. John wrote that the blood of Jesus has purified us from all sin (see 1 John 1:7).

Finally, Jesus has redeemed us from a future of eternal damnation, or hell. He purchased our redemption with His blood sacrifice: "You were bought at a price" (1 Corinthians 6:20). By believing in Jesus, we are guaranteed an eternal future in heaven.

Different religions have different means of salvation. Are they all valid in their own way, or is there just one Savior and just one path to salvation? The words of Acts 4:12 brook no argument: Jesus is *the* Savior. We need to know God's Word so we won't be misled. And we need to know Jesus to be saved.

SECOND ADAM

The first man is of the earth, earthy;
the second man is the Lord from heaven.
1 CORINTHIANS 15:47 KJV

The beginning of the downfall of humankind can be traced to Adam and to his single desire: He wanted to be like God. It didn't take much tempting from the evil one, disguised as a serpent, to get the first man to eat from the forbidden tree so that he could supposedly "be like God" (see Genesis 3:1–6).

Like Adam, Jesus—who has been called the Second Adam—was a living being. But Jesus was also what Adam was not and could never be: He was God in the flesh. Jesus, Paul wrote, "being in very nature God, did not consider equality with God something to be grasped" (Philippians 2:6).

Because of Adam's fall, sin entered the world, resulting in death for all who chronologically followed him. Because of the Second Adam's resurrection, death is not the final chapter for believers: "For as in Adam all die, so in Christ all will be made alive" (1 Corinthians 15:22).

It's a bit of an understatement, but Adam made a poor choice in the Garden of Eden. When you think about it, though, his choice is like many we face. Will we honor God or won't we? Will we follow Jesus, the Second Adam? We *are* responsible for the choices we make.

SEED OF ABRAHAM

The promises were spoken to Abraham and to his seed. The Scripture does not say "and to seeds," meaning many people, but "and to your seed," meaning one person, who is Christ.
GALATIANS 3:16

The Galatians, formerly a pagan people—and like many new Christians—were eager to learn but not always so discerning. Since the time when Paul had led them to Christ, they had been influenced by other interpreters of the faith and now Paul needed to set the record straight.

Some of these interpreters were known as "Judaizers," or Jewish Christians who believed that in order to be saved, certain aspects of Mosaic law had to be followed as well as Jesus' teachings. To counter such theories, Paul went to the heart of the matter: Who is Jesus, and who are Jesus' followers?

First, he said, Jesus is the natural descendant, or seed, of Abraham (see Matthew 1). But Paul went further: Jesus, as the seed of Abraham, is the fulfillment of God's covenant. That meant that all people of all nations, including the Galatians, would be blessed through Jesus (see Genesis 12:3). If you have faith in Jesus, Paul said, you are Abraham's seed, too (see Galatians 3:29), and have been freed from having to follow the rituals of the law.

Jesus doesn't care where or if we went to college, and He isn't fazed by our club memberships, stock portfolio, or familial pedigree. Moreover, He is blind to the color of our skin and our ethnic and religious background. To Him, the Seed of Abraham, we are all precious in His sight.

SEED OF THE WOMAN

And I will put enmity between you and the woman, and between your offspring and hers; he will crush your head, and you will strike his heel.
GENESIS 3:15

Before issuing His punishment of Adam and Eve, who had just eaten the forbidden fruit, God delivered a stinging, prophetic rebuke to the serpent. God sentenced the creature to a future of crawling on its belly and eating dust. And God sentenced Satan, who inhabited the creature, to a future of struggle, ending with his ultimate defeat (crushed) by the seed of the woman.

Jesus would be the offspring or seed of the woman, born on earth to a virgin and to a Father who was God. During Jesus' time on earth, Satan would repeatedly "strike his heel," or attempt to hurt Him, but he would not succeed. When Jesus rose from the dead after three days in the tomb, He effectively "crushed the head" of Satan by defeating death and overcoming the power of sin. (Scholars have noted that while striking someone's heel is painful, it is not a life-threatening injury. On the other hand, crushing someone's head is usually fatal.) When Jesus returns a second time to establish His kingdom, He will vanquish Satan forever (see Revelation 20:1–10). As Paul wrote, "The God of peace will soon crush Satan under your feet" (Romans 16:20).

Evil forces continue to surround and torment us, and Christians especially are under attack around the world. Remember the missionaries and Christians who live where Christianity is not tolerated in your prayers and take heart from Paul's words in Romans 8:31: "If God is for us, who can be against us?"

SERVANT

Behold my servant, whom I uphold; mine elect, in whom
my soul delighteth; I have put my spirit upon him:
he shall bring forth judgment to the Gentiles.
ISAIAH 42:1 KJV

Not only did Isaiah predict the eventual result of Jesus'
servant ministry—that the Gentiles would be reached—but
he also described His servant attitude. Isaiah wrote that Jesus
would be "led like a lamb to the slaughter" (Isaiah 53:7), a
reference to His obedience to His Father by submitting to a
most brutal and painful death. Mark, the gospel writer, also
commented on this: "For even the Son of Man did not come
to be served, but to serve, and to give his life as a ransom for
many" (Mark 10:45).

Jesus as Servant may be most clearly seen when He
washed the feet of His disciples during the serving of the
Last Supper (see John 13:1–20). When Peter told Him that
He would never wash his feet, Jesus replied, "Unless I wash
you, you have no part with me" (verse 8). When He finished
washing their feet, Jesus told His disciples that He had done
it so that they could go and do likewise.

Being a servant, or displaying such servantlike qualities as
meekness and humility, was also threaded throughout Jesus'
sermons. Jesus praised the "poor in spirit" and the "meek" (see
Matthew 5:3–5), advocated loving and praying for your enemy
(5:44), and extolled giving anonymously to the needy (6:3).

We're expected to follow Jesus' example—but how exactly do we serve God? There is nothing we can give or do for God because He created everything. Peter, having learned the hard way about obedience, supplied the answer: "If anyone serves, he should do it with the strength God provides, so that in all things God may be praised through Jesus Christ" (1 Peter 4:11). We serve God by praising Jesus. . .servants praising the Servant.

SHEPHERD

For you were like sheep going astray, but now you have
returned to the Shepherd and Overseer of your souls.
1 PETER 2:25

Jesus had once told Peter to "feed my sheep" (see John
21:17)—and now the disciple was doing just that. Writing to
Jewish Christians who had fled Jerusalem because of intense
persecution, Peter encouraged them about how to live during
difficult times. Perhaps because Jesus had often referred to
Himself as a Shepherd, Peter also described his Lord as such,
as the One who would lead His people to greener pastures
and still waters.

In this passage, the words "Shepherd and Overseer" come
from the Greek *poimen kai episkopos*, which can be translated
"Guardian Shepherd." Not only does Jesus as Shepherd care
for and feed His sheep, He also protects them.

Jesus showed His compassion time and again, whether
by healing and restoring to life or by His words. His parable
of the Good Samaritan who goes out of his way to show
abundant mercy is an illustration of Jesus Himself (see Luke
10:25–37). When Jesus saw the five thousand gathered to see
Him, "he had compassion on them, because they were like
sheep without a shepherd" (Mark 6:34). To those people, and
to all who read His Word, Jesus feeds His flock with living
water and the bread of life (see John 4).

When He walked the earth, Jesus demonstrated His

desire to protect His followers. Praying to God the Father shortly before His arrest, Jesus said of His disciples, "While I was with them, I protected them and kept them safe by that name you gave me" (John 17:12). And speaking of the Jewish people whom He had come to save and who rejected Him, Jesus said, "How often I have longed to gather your children together, as a hen gathers her chicks under her wings, but you were not willing!" (Luke 13:34).

Having ascended to heaven, Jesus is now the ultimate Shepherd, not allowing anything—"neither death nor life, neither angels nor demons, neither the present nor the future, nor any powers, neither height nor depth, nor anything else in all creation" (Romans 8:38–39)—to separate His believers from His love.

Most of us are not being persecuted for our faith. But that doesn't mean we don't need a Shepherd. While not often life-threatening, what's going on in our daily existence can be unsettling to say the least. Seek Jesus' plan for your life and ask Him to protect your paths—and then wait and listen.

SHILOH

*The sceptre shall not depart from Judah, nor a lawgiver
from between his feet, until Shiloh come; and unto
him shall the gathering of the people be.*
GENESIS 49:10 KJV

Jacob's final prophetic blessing to his sons, whose names became those of the twelve tribes of Israel, contains many enigmatic passages. The most detailed blessing was bestowed on Judah, from which tribe Jesus' earthly parents were descended.

Shiloh, which has been translated as "to whom dominion belongs" or "resting place," or as a derivative of Shalom ("Peaceful One"), is the Messiah or Jesus. When Jesus began His ministry on earth, He declared Himself the Son of God and acknowledged His authority as such (John 5:16–27). At the end of His earthly ministry, He declared, "All authority in heaven and on earth has been given to me" (Matthew 28:18).

The scepter of Judah, recognized by scholars as the tribal identity, and in particular, the right of the tribe to impose capital punishment, did not depart from Judah until the first century AD, corresponding with the arrival of Jesus.

While crowds in Galilee gathered to hear Jesus wherever He went, one day, when He returns, He will rule an eternal kingdom and be lauded as the King of kings (see Revelation 21). In the resting place of Shiloh, the New Jerusalem, peace will reign at last.

Jacob could not have known the exact meaning of his farewell messages to his sons. The words he spoke were divinely inspired by God so that seeds would be planted and hopes would be raised of the Messiah to come. God wanted there to be no doubt that when Jesus did come, He alone fulfilled every ancient prophecy. Rest assured that Shiloh is Jesus, and that Jesus is the Son of God.

SON OF DAVID

And, behold, a woman of Canaan. . .cried unto him, saying,
Have mercy on me, O Lord, thou son of David.
MATTHEW 15:22 KJV

The woman had been pestering the disciples and they wanted to be rid of her. But she wouldn't stop crying out for Jesus. She wouldn't stop because she had been pushed to the edge, having to deal with a daughter suffering from demon possession. Her faith had led her to Jesus, and because of her deep convictions, she addressed Him as the Son of David.

More than a thousand years earlier, the prophet Nathan had told King David that God would establish the eternal throne of one of his offspring (see 2 Samuel 7:13). God had said of this king, "I will be his father, and he will be my son" (verse 14). The prophet Jeremiah had also foretold that this Son of David would be a "righteous Branch sprout[ed] from David's line" (Jeremiah 33:15). Such prophecies, fulfilled upon Jesus' birth, were confirmed in the genealogies found in the gospels of Matthew and Luke.

Jesus didn't go to the Canaanite woman's house and lay His hands on her daughter. He merely praised the woman's great faith and said that her request was granted. From that very hour, her daughter was healed. Have you exercised your faith today? Jesus, the Son of David, wants us to *trust* in Him.

SON OF GOD

The angel answered, "The Holy Spirit will come upon you, and the power of the Most High will overshadow you. So the holy one to be born will be called the Son of God."

LUKE 1:35

Even though Jesus was born of Mary, who received this pronouncement from the angel, He was conceived by the Holy Spirit. In other words, Jesus is God in human form. And because He was from God and of God, He was heralded as the Son of God.

While righteous followers of Jesus have been described as sons of God (see Matthew 5:9), and believers have been designated as children of God (see John 1:12), there is only one unique Son of God. The words "only begotten" from John 3:16 (KJV)—"For God so loved the world, that he gave his only begotten Son"—come from the Greek *monogenes*, which means "one of a kind." Only the Son of God could have the same nature as God, could demonstrate unearthly power, and could have been resurrected from the dead.

Jesus has been described as "the radiance of God's glory and the exact representation of his being" (Hebrews 1:3). So, it follows that Jesus, as the Son, has seen God. John wrote, "No one has ever seen God, but God the One and Only, who is at the Father's side, has made him known" (John 1:18). Only Jesus, the Son of God, is seated at the right hand of God (see Colossians 3:1).

Because God put all things under His power (see John 13:3), Jesus was able to perform feats never before witnessed on earth: He stilled the wind and the waves; He walked on water; He turned water into wine; He fed thousands with a few loaves and fish (and had leftovers!); He healed the lame, blind, demon-possessed, and ill; and He raised people from the dead.

More than those extraordinary acts, though, Jesus proved that He was the Son of God by being resurrected from the dead (see Romans 1:4). By taking all of humankind's wrongdoing with Him to the cross, dying for the sins of the world, and then overcoming the power of sin by rising from the dead, He saved His believers from God's judgment and eternal damnation.

Why did Jesus come to earth as the Son of God? The story of His disciple Thomas provides some insight. While some of the other disciples had encountered Jesus after the resurrection, Thomas hadn't actually seen the Lord for himself. Stubbornly, he declared that unless he saw the nail marks in Jesus' hands and side, he wouldn't believe that Jesus had risen from the dead. A week later, Jesus faced him in person and said, "Stop doubting and believe" (John 20:27).

Because of the miracle of the resurrection, and because of all that Jesus said and did, we can have faith that He is who He says He is. By coming to earth, Jesus proved that God exists and that He is the Son of God. Stop doubting and believe.

SON OF MAN

For the Son of man is come to save that which was lost.
MATTHEW 18:11 KJV

In the Bible, the name "Son of Man" is used to describe Jesus around eighty times. In Matthew 18, Jesus was teaching because the disciples had asked Him who would be the greatest in heaven. Jesus said that those who possess a childlike faith will enter the kingdom of heaven and those who humble themselves will be the greatest. Jesus referred to Himself as the Son of Man because He, too, was human (the Son of Man is, after all, a man) and He understood them. Moreover, He was the perfect representation of humility. (This name was also used by God when addressing the prophet Ezekiel.)

"Son of Man" was also used to proclaim Jesus as Messiah. In one of the visions given him by God of the end times, the prophet Daniel described "one like a son of man, coming with the clouds of heaven. . . . He was given authority, glory and sovereign power; all peoples, nations and men of every language worshiped him" (Daniel 7:13–14). As the Son of Man, Jesus also evoked these images (see Matthew 24:27–44) while describing how He would have to suffer, die, and be resurrected to fulfill prophecies made only of the Messiah.

Anyone who's lived with a teenager has probably heard these words: "You just don't understand me!" That excuse won't work with Jesus. As the Son of Man, and the Son of God, Jesus knows inside and out the trials of the human condition. He's been there and done that. When we follow Him, He wants to help us lead the best life that's humanly possible.

SON OF MARY

Is not this the carpenter, the son of Mary. . . ?
And they were offended at him.
MARK 6:3 KJV

The people of Nazareth certainly weren't looking at the larger picture. They couldn't separate their idea of who Jesus was—local carpenter and son of Mary—from the man He had become. How could a boy raised in a dusty village possess such knowledge? How could He perform miracles?

Little is known of Mary, save her role as the vessel for the birth of God's Son, Jesus. She was of the tribe of Judah and a relative of Elizabeth, the mother of John the Baptist. Mary was the only person to have been with Jesus from His birth to His death on earth.

By the time Jesus came to Nazareth's synagogue, Mary was probably a widow since there is no mention of Jesus being Joseph's son. She was blessed to have a large family, giving birth to four more sons and some daughters after Jesus. She was at the cross when Jesus was crucified and then afterward went to live with the disciple John.

Who is Jesus to you? Like the people of Nazareth in

Jesus' day, we sometimes assign Jesus a role and refuse to see Him as He really is. Yes, He was the Son of Mary, but more importantly, He is the Son of God, the Creator of the earth, and the King of kings and Lord of lords. He is worthy of our highest praise, our utmost reverence, and our undying devotion.

SON OF THE MOST HIGH

*"He will be great and will be called
the Son of the Most High."*
LUKE 1:32

Hearing those words, Mary must have trembled. Of all the women in the world, God, the Most High, had chosen her to bear His Son. This precious baby, who would grow in her womb and to whom she would give birth, would be called the Son of the Most High.

In the Old Testament, God the Father is frequently referred to as the Most High. The psalmist wrote, "For you, O LORD, are the Most High over all the earth; you are exalted far above all gods" (Psalm 97:9). In the New Testament, Jesus is acknowledged as the Son of the Most High only twice: by the angel Gabriel and by a demon-possessed man who lived in the tombs near the Sea of Galilee (see Luke 8:26–39). Seeing Jesus, the man cried out, "What do you want with me, Jesus, Son of the Most High God?" Jesus proceeded to send the demons out of the man and into a herd of pigs which then ran off a cliff and drowned.

Proudly announced by an angel and fearfully declared by a legion of demons, Jesus is truly the Son of the Most High.

Every believer has a role to play in God's kingdom. We may not be missionary material or pulpit prospects, but Jesus has chosen us to serve Him, the Son of the Most High, in some way. Pray to be led. . .and then be prepared to follow.

SPIRIT OF TRUTH

"But when he, the Spirit of truth, comes,
he will guide you into all truth."
JOHN 16:13

The disciples were understandably depressed. For more than three years they had followed Jesus faithfully, trying (often unsuccessfully) to grasp His concepts, and now He was telling them that He was leaving. Why was He going when there was so much more to do in Galilee? And how could they carry on without Him?

Recognizing that the disciples had enough to deal with at present—they didn't need to know the details of His departure—Jesus offered these words of comfort. Yes, He was going away, but the Spirit of Truth, which is really Jesus' Spirit, would come to them and live inside of them. He would never leave them "as orphans" because He would always be with them (see John 14:15–19).

The truth of Jesus' words wouldn't become clear until after His death, resurrection, and ascension. On the day of Pentecost, ten days after Jesus' ascension, the disciples were filled with the Holy Spirit, the Spirit of Truth. They were then able, because of the guiding of the Spirit of Truth, to spread the gospel, perform miracles in Jesus' name, and write their accounts of Jesus' ministry (see Ephesians 3:5).

In Old Testament times, the Spirit of Truth also guided the words of the prophets: "No prophecy of Scripture came about by the prophet's own interpretation. For prophecy never had its origin in the will of man, but men spoke from God as they were carried along by the Holy Spirit" (2 Peter 1:20–21).

Because of Jesus' promise to the disciples, all believers in Him continue to receive the gift of the Spirit of Truth. How do we know that we are being guided by the Holy Spirit? Only the Spirit of Truth acknowledges that Jesus came to earth; the others are from the evil one (see 1 John 4:1–6). The power to overcome evil comes only from the Spirit of Truth: "The one who is in you is greater than the one who is in the world" (1 John 4:4).

The self-help section in bookstores is overflowing with books designed to help you love yourself—and then go on to amazing personal relationships and careers. But instead of turning to ourselves for help, why not seek the source of all truth and strength? When you follow Jesus, only then can you look inside yourself and find help—because the Spirit of Truth is there.

SUN OF RIGHTEOUSNESS

But unto you that fear my name shall the Sun of righteousness
arise with healing in his wings; and ye shall go forth,
and grow up as calves of the stall.
MALACHI 4:2 KJV

Jesus said that He is the light of the world—and many of His names attest to this. From the days of the early church, the name "Sun of Righteousness" referred to Jesus, a name that had been prophesied four hundred years before Jesus' birth in Bethlehem.

When John the Baptist was born, his father, Zechariah, filled with the Holy Spirit, praised "the tender mercy of our God, by which the rising sun will come to us from heaven to shine on those living in darkness" (Luke 1:78–79). He was speaking of Jesus, whose ministry would be preceded by that of John the Baptist.

Since Jesus came to earth, the Sun of Righteousness has risen and has been shining continuously. Like the rays emanating from the sun, Jesus' healing powers have touched countless souls, making them whole. The light that He radiates is greater than any darkness: When we are in His presence, He shows the way to go. That way is the way to freedom from the oppressive realm of sin.

At times, the forces of evil surrounding us are almost palpable. When those feelings arise, call upon the name of Jesus. Say His name until His peace surrounds you. Say His name until you feel the Sun of Righteousness shine down on you.

TEACHER

*He replied, "Go into the city to a certain man and tell him,
'The Teacher says: My appointed time is near. I am going to
celebrate the Passover with my disciples at your house.'"*

MATTHEW 26:18

There was no need for further clarification. For the last three years—in the temple in Jerusalem, in the synagogues of Galilee, and from hillsides and in boats—one Teacher, Jesus, had astounded the people with His message. He taught in parables, and His words often confused and confounded His listeners. And all along the way, He was preparing His disciples to continue His ministry.

The prophet Isaiah had foretold Jesus' great skills as the Teacher: "The Spirit of the LORD will rest on him—the Spirit of wisdom and of understanding, the Spirit of counsel and of power, the Spirit of knowledge and of the fear of the LORD—and he will delight in the fear of the LORD" (Isaiah 11:2–3).

When He taught, the people were amazed because He taught them from a position of authority—not like the teachers of the law (see Mark 1:22). They wondered where He got His wisdom (see Mark 6:2), and they wondered at His message. Who before Jesus had said "The first shall be last" or that the meek would inherit the earth? Who before Jesus had said that, upon believing in Him, thieves, prostitutes, and sinners of all kinds would be welcomed in heaven? Only God's Son, Jesus, the Teacher, could impart such wisdom.

We can't join the crowds on a Galilean hillside to hear Jesus—but that doesn't mean He's not still teaching us. He still instructs us through His Word, the Bible. And, every day, He still sends people and opportunities into our lives to guide us and, in the process, draw us closer to Himself. We just have to be paying attention.

VINE

I am the true vine, and my Father is the husbandman.
JOHN 15:1 KJV

Jesus probably spoke these words while He and the disciples were still sitting at the table of the Last Supper, the goblets that held wine in full view. Jesus knew the analogy was particularly apt. In ancient Israel, winemaking was one of the pillars of the economy. Healthy vines were much prized, and able husbandmen, or vine dressers, were in demand.

Jesus was going away—to be crucified and then to return to heaven—and the disciples needed something to cling to. They needed to know that Jesus was the Vine and God was the husbandman. They needed to know that they were branches of that vine and that only as they stayed closely connected to Him (like a branch to a vine) would His life flow through them and bear fruit by bringing others to know Him.

How were they to abide in the Vine? Jesus told them to abide in His words, to remember what He taught them; to abide in His love and to love others as He loved them; and to obey His teaching. Later, the disciples would realize the heartbreaking reality of His words: "Greater love has no one than this, that he lay down his life for his friends" (John 15:13).

Sports enthusiasts talk about "getting in the game"—playing the sport, knowing the rules and the teams, being part of the action. How about "getting in the Vine"? You can't be an effective Sunday school teacher, Bible study leader, or witness unless that's where you are. . .learning, loving, and obeying Jesus.

THE WAY, THE TRUTH, AND THE LIFE

Jesus saith unto him, I am the way, the truth, and the life: no man cometh unto the Father, but by me.
JOHN 14:6 KJV

Time was running out for Jesus' ministry on earth and also for Jesus to make sure the disciples really knew who He was. While they were sharing the Last Supper, which would be their final meal together before Jesus' crucifixion, Jesus told the disciples again that He was going away and that He would prepare a place for them to join Him. Thomas responded by saying the disciples didn't know where He was going, and, besides, how could they join Him since they don't know the way?

In response, Jesus made things simple. He told them that He was the Way, the Truth, and the Life.

Jesus had taught earlier about the way to heaven. "For wide is the gate and broad is the road that leads to destruction, and many enter through it. But small is the gate and narrow the road that leads to life, and only a few find it" (Matthew 7:13–14). There are two roads (ways) to travel in life, but only one leads to heaven. That way is marked by sacrifice, commitment, and belief in Jesus (see Luke 9:23). That Way is Jesus.

While talking to some Jewish people who believed in Him, Jesus said that if they held to His teachings, they would know the truth and that truth would set them free (see John 8:32). Later, when He prayed to the Father for His disciples, Jesus said, "Sanctify them by the truth; your word is truth" (John 17:17). As John declared early in his gospel account, Jesus is the Word (see John 1:1); therefore, Jesus is the Truth.

Jesus was not only offering eternal life to His disciples; He was declaring Himself as the source of life. Indeed, John described Jesus as the Creator, saying, "Through him all things were made; without him nothing was made that has been made. In Him was life, and that life was the light of men" (John 1:3–4). Paul wrote that Jesus "is before all things, and in him all things hold together" (Colossians 1:17).

Because Jesus is the Way, the Truth, and the Life, He is the Savior. Only He has the power to offer salvation for sin; only He has the power to give eternal life. As Jesus said, "I have come that they may have life, and have it to the full" (John 10:10).

Some choices in life you make without thinking—or, rather, without thinking of the consequences. Those are the kind of choices littered alongside the broad road, the road Jesus spoke of that doesn't lead to life. On that road, travelers simply satisfy their senses for immediate gratification. To travel on the other road, one must understand, accept, and believe, and then live by faith. Life isn't easy, but it is fulfilling when you follow Jesus. Just as He wanted the disciples to know, Jesus wants you to know who He is—and why you believe what you do.

WONDERFUL COUNSELOR

For to us a child is born, to us a son is given,
and the government will be on his shoulders.
And he will be called Wonderful Counselor.
ISAIAH 9:6

Isaiah had tried to get King Ahaz to listen to him. With Assyria threatening Judah, the king was in a dire situation and he desperately needed God's wisdom and counsel. But unlike his predecessor, King Uzziah, King Ahaz was an evil ruler who ultimately went his own way—with predictably disastrous results. Even though Judah formed a coalition with Assyria, in short order, Assyria conquered them, taking their people captive. Isaiah described Judah's people then as "distressed and hungry. . .[who] looking upward, will curse their king and their God" (Isaiah 8:21).

Suddenly, into this dark and murky milieu came a ray of inexplicable, incomprehensible brightness. Despite Ahaz's obstinance, and that of generations of kings before him, God had not forgotten His people. A child was to be born. . .a child that would rescue God's people. The word that was translated as "wonderful" also means "beyond understanding." And the word "counselor" doesn't mean a lawyer, psychologist, or therapist. Rather, the word was initially used to describe a military strategist.

Still, as Jesus began His ministry, He quickly gained a reputation as a man of compassion and someone who keenly understood the human condition. John wrote, "He did not need man's testimony about man, for he knew what was in a man" (John 2:25). He suffered humiliation and pain; He experienced joy and peace. Indeed, His purpose in becoming a man was so He could help those "who are being tempted" (Hebrews 2:18). Jesus knew that the world is overwhelming at times and that, because of sin, we all need to have a relationship with Him.

And how does Jesus serve as a Wonderful Counselor? By asking us to trust in Him. Only Jesus has overcome the world; only Jesus has power over sin and death. He has never turned away those who earnestly seek Him. When we love Jesus, we obey His teachings (see John 14:24)—and in turn, begin to lead a better life.

Like King Ahaz, we often want to do things our own way. After covering all the bases and considering all the outcomes, we usually come to one conclusion—our own. But we all need a Wonderful Counselor, and we all need His guidance. To exclude God from our decisions is to deny Him lordship of our lives. Remember: Nothing is too hard for Jesus.

WORD

In the beginning was the Word,
and the Word was with God, and the Word was God.
JOHN 1:1 KJV

Bible scholars have said that Matthew's gospel shows that Jesus is the Messiah, Mark's account points to Jesus as the Servant, and Luke reveals Jesus as a man. John, though, describes Jesus as God—and he gets to the point right away.

Jesus is the Word, which is translated from the Greek word *logos*, a word that can also mean "wisdom." To the ancients, words were the personification of their speakers, being considered almost living beings. They had no trouble believing that God is the Word, and several verses from the Old Testament attest to this: "By the word of the LORD were the heavens made; their starry host by the breath of his mouth" (Psalm 33:6); "He sent forth his word and healed them" (Psalm 107:20); "So is my word that goes out from my mouth: It will not return to me empty" (Isaiah 55:11); and "Is not my word like fire. . .and like a hammer that breaks a rock in pieces?" (Jeremiah 23:29).

The New Testament Greeks believed that Jesus as logos was a bridge between God and His creation. In other words, Jesus was the mediator between heaven and earth. The New Testament Hebrews, on the other hand, believed that Jesus as logos was the thinker and the eternal Creator. John incorporated both of these viewpoints into his gospel.

John's gospel account shows that because Jesus is the Word, and the Word has always been God, then Jesus is God. Thus, every characteristic of Jesus is a reflection of God, and every word that He spoke came from God. Hear the power of the Word in these verses spoken by Jesus: "For God so loved the world that he gave his one and only Son, that whoever believes in him shall not perish but have eternal life" (John 3:16); and "I tell you the truth, whoever hears my word and believes him who sent me has eternal life and will not be condemned; he has crossed over from death to life" (John 5:24).

The Word has the power of life, eternal life, but the Word is also spirit. Jesus said, "The Spirit gives life; the flesh counts for nothing. The words I have spoken to you are spirit and they are life" (John 6:63). The Word was not revealed by the wisdom of men and women but only by the Holy Spirit, who is Jesus. Without the Word, there would be no Christian faith, no Holy Spirit, and no eternal life.

The Word is also the essence of truth—and there is only one standard for truth. Scholars point to the Greek letter *omicron* preceding the word *logos* as evidence that the writer meant *the* Word (as opposed to *a* Word). When Jesus prayed for His disciples, He said, "Sanctify them by the truth; your word is truth" (John 17:17). And when Jesus testified in front of Pontius Pilate, He said, "For this reason I was born, and for this I came into the world, to testify to the truth" (John 18:37). Every word spoken by Jesus, by God, is true and can be trusted.

It's fitting that "The Word" be the last name of God in this book, because that name is truly the summation of everything He is. In the beginning was the Word. . .and, when the world as we know it no longer exists, the Word will rule when Jesus reigns over the New Jerusalem. The Word announced His birth; was the witness of His ministry; and brought the message of salvation to a world covered in darkness. The Word is comfort and consolation, gift, guide, and refuge. The Word is a rock, the foundation of our faith, and through its teaching, the path to the Way, the Truth, and the Life. The Word is God speaking to you.

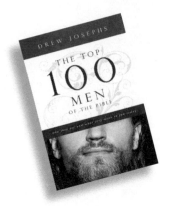
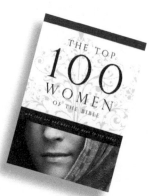
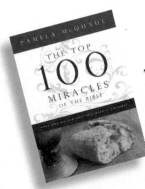